MY JOURNEY AND MY STORY

Memoirs of My Life

EVANGELIST
DIANE CARROLL

My Journey and My Story

Memoirs of My Life

By Evangelist Diane Cheak Carroll

Cover Designed by Anelda L. Attaway

Published by Jazzy Kitty Publications

Logo Designed by Justin Ackerman

Editor: Anelda L. Attaway

© 2024 Diane Carroll

ISBN 978-1-954425-86-6

Library of Congress Control Number: 2024902236

ACKNOWLEDGMENTS

I want to acknowledge my friend, Shirley Corsey, who after many interesting conversations, asked me, "Why don't you write a book about your experiences?" Surprisingly, I had never considered writing a book, yet I loved to read books and have been inspired by others. The seed that Shirley planted has grown into a reality and I am so thankful for her encouraging me to share my story. She inspired me to tell others what they too can do when they keep their eye on the prize and see God move in their life.

To my good friend, Ella Davis, who has listened to my story and cheers me on to share the blessings and memories that will strengthen others to share how they achieved their dreams.

To my special friend, Penny Martin, who knows how to help me clarify my thoughts and dispel any confusion in writing my story. She makes it easy to remove the barriers and forge ahead in sharing my experiences in a smooth, clear way whenever I have been overwhelmed in writing.

Lastly, I thank my husband, Sumblar B. Carroll, for sharing his time and suggestions by supporting me as I share my life experiences with others. I know others will be blessed and inspired as I share my journey.

DEDICATIONS

To My Wonderful Parents:

Rev. Eugene Henry Cheak

and

Ruth Brown Cheak

My Daughters:

SeLiques Diane Simmons

and

April Allexis Lindsey

My Grandchildren:

Courtney SeLiques Carroll, Saqqara Iman Carroll,

Kendal Corinne Simmons

Autumn Skye Carroll-Lindsey

and

Lloyal Theodore Sumblar Lindsey

TABLE OF CONTENTS

Introduction - Birth...i

Living on New Street...01

Prejudice Among Us..04

Quinton Fire..05

Tree of Prayer...07

Fun Times with Friends..09

At the Supper Table...10

Home Life on New Street..15

Dancing and Prancing..17

Our Fights and Discord..20

Parents Working Hard on New Street...................................22

My Parents...25

Brothers and Sisters..36

Church and Our Faith...44

Christmas at Our House..50

The New Year Parade...53

Visiting Grandpop Brown..55

Ride of Faith..58

Family Hardship – Baby Brother Michael..............................62

Senior Year in High School...66

First Prom..68

After Graduation – Salem Technical Institute........................71

TABLE OF CONTENTS

Prayer Answered...73

Cumberland College 77

College Graduation 79

Teacher's Job, New Home, and Moving to Delaware 81

Meeting My Husband 85

Engaged 89

The Wedding Day...91

Back to Work 93

What? Moving to Our Apartment.......................96

Searching to Buy a New Home 98

Our Dream Home..100

Moving in Our Dream Home...............................103

Back to College 105

Jobless but Not Hopeless...................................108

St. Francis Hospital...110

Earning My Bachelor's and Master's Degrees.....112

Neighborhood House...114

Porter State Service Center...............................116

Remembering the Blessings from God.................119

The Cheak Family Tree 122

About the Author...123

I t was a rainy night on November 5, 1947, when my mother, Ruth, told me that my father rushed her to Salem Hospital because she was in labor with me. Mom said labor was agonizing and long but finally right at 7:07 p.m. I was born to her and my father, Eugene. It had been four years since my sister, Naomi, was born and I was the fourth child of 7 children delivered into the Cheak family. Mom smiled as she told me my father proudly named me Dianna Barbara Cheak, although everyone else called me Diane. However, I noticed whenever my father called me or wanted to get my attention, he called me Dianna and that made me feel like he was calling me "Queen Dianna" to him. I am so blessed that the Lord placed me in the Cheak family where I felt safe, happy and most of all loved. I am so thankful that Mom shared my birth story with me.

Now in my Golden years, memories that I alone have experienced constantly come to mind. I now feel compelled to share with my children, grandchildren, and friends to reveal parts of our family legacy. I realized that If I don't share my stories they will never be told. My journey of faith has blessed me and kept me through the highs and lows of my life. That is why I give all the praise and all the glory to our Lord and Savior, Jesus Christ!

I want to share my experiences with you as my parents shared their faith, struggles, and dreams with me. May my journey help you along the way to obey, serve, and trust our Lord and Savior.

<u>LIVING ON NEW STREET</u>

B ack in the 1950s and '60s, New Street was the main place where almost all Black folks lived in Quinton, New Jersey. Many families on New Street went to church which was a way of life for most of us. Most families got along and it seemed like a little village to me. During those times, parents stuck together in instructing the right and wrongs for the children too. Most of the children on New Street respected the adults and they knew not to talk back or be disrespectful to adults or they would get in trouble when they got home. Now there were a chosen few troublemakers but they were dealt with accordingly.

Each of the 21 houses on New Street had a big, beautiful tree in the front yard that leaned toward the center of the street, appearing like an arched bridge covering from one side of the street to the other. During the summers, the large green trees gave cool shade to the neighbors as cars slowly drove through our street on a hot summer day. During those times, most of us did not have air conditioners.

Often, the tomato trucks stopped at the end of the street, all of us would run and take as many tomatoes as possible off the back of the truck, then we ran back home to sit on the front steps enjoying the juicy tomatoes with salt. Sometimes, we even made tomato sandwiches as we sat and filled our stomachs while others talked about how many tomatoes they took off the truck. Those were the innocent times on New Street. We knew how to have fun in simple ways.

During the summer, we would often see friends sitting on the front steps talking or playing a game of jacks, monopoly, marbles, or the ice pick challenges. There were about 90 to 100 children on our street and everyone knew each other. Now and then the whole neighborhood would play baseball together in the middle of the street.

There was respect for each other on New Street and when I think back, we had something very special that carried me through life. We were blessed with things that were far beyond money and riches. I loved living on New Street because we had things you could not buy like good relationships and families that stuck together. The love and respect went a long way in teaching us to work together. Those were the special times and blessings we all enjoyed.

At night, there was only one large streetlight on our street and we would play Tag, Hide and Go See, and other games under the streetlight. The games were fun and little did I know how much it helped us learn to get along with others and how to follow the rules of the game. Many families became friends and socialized with one another, which is much different from the cell phones and other electrical gadgets people use today. I realized that rules were followed to help us grow and mature in learning how to handle differences.

I realize that New Street was a good place to grow up in a very healthy and godly way. There were hard-working and religious parents who were caring and stuck together in raising the children in the right way. We children never realized how poor we were as we enjoyed the simple games and fun times we had together and we knew the difference between fair and unfair in our dealings. There was no teasing and putting down others or acting like your family was better than other families on New Street.

<u>PREJUDICE AMONG US</u>

I remember in the early 1960s, when I was around 13 years old there were many disputes regarding school desegregation. Much anger arose among the Whites who did not want Blacks to integrate with schools. However, to my surprise, one Noonday about 15 carloads full of White men drove down New Street and they stopped right in the middle of the street, then all of the White men got out of their cars with bats in their hands and shouted racial slurs, warning us "Niggers" to stay in our place and stay segregated as it was.

Everyone on our street stood shocked as we never bothered them. But much fear and anger were felt by us all as we stood in shock with no response to them. Then the White men got back into their cars and drove away.

I felt not only fear but anger and disrespect that they thought they were better than us just because of the color of their skin. I knew that was wrong because God doesn't make one color better than another. God made only one Human Race. I was glad I knew the Lord because I prayed and I knew our God would take care of it all. They never returned but we understood how they felt about us.

QUINTON FIRE

Sometime after that incident, early one April morning, when there was great unrest and conflicts in public opinions and discord was still in the air.

The wind blew and suddenly there was a fire on Main Street. The fire whistle blew and there was a huge fire in Schmidt's Lumber yard! The fire raged and the wind blew furiously! Suddenly the Post Office was on fire, then Nettie's Grocery Store caught fire, and then Hayes Toy Shop. Black smoke was everywhere as the fire jumped from one home to another. Suddenly, the homes on the other streets were also going up in flames.

I could not believe there was fire everywhere! It was frightening! I immediately ran around the corner to Main Street and I looked in horror as it looked like the whole world was on fire! I sat crying my eyes out, I could not believe Quinton was burning down. Immediately, I ran back home and all of New Street was standing with the wind moving in the opposite direction fueling the fire on Main Street, while New Street was safe and unaffected.

Other Fire Departments came to assist the huge fires in Quinton and when it was all over, Main Street and almost all the stores were burnt to the ground. New Street was unharmed.

Afterward, many White people complained, "Saying, that it should it have been New Street to burn down!" We stood in silence at the nerve of them saying that New Street should have been burned down and not Main Street. Bitterness was in the air.

But just like all kinds of weather happen all over the world, it is God alone who controls everything and man is limited when it comes to God's creation. God has a reason and a purpose for everything in His creation. But one thing I know, God wants us all to have love and compassion for each other.

Meanwhile, Main Street was rebuilt, but I doubt New Street would have been. It's situations and things like this I talked to God about as I sat up in my tree next to the kitchen to pray.

There were many changes which were contrary to the Word of God. During that time divorces were rare and looked down upon and so was "shacking up" which was living together and being unmarried. People lived conservatively and expressed nonbiblical views. Yes, in the 1960s many changes were going on in the world.

TREE OF PRAYER

O ften, I loved to climb the tree next to the kitchen door. I would often sit high in that tree so no one saw me to be alone and talk with God about my thoughts and desires. I often felt like God and I had a special place for me to pray.

When I was lonely, I would sit and watch family and friends go in and out the kitchen door as the young children came to buy the best ice cream in Quinton. My father made and sold homemade ice cream to the neighborhood children for 5 cents a comb. Dad would have us take turns for hours to churn the delicious homemade ice cream. Every child on New Street loved Dad's ice cream as they ran to our house every time they got 5 cents to buy an ice cream comb. My dad saved so many coins that he filled gallons and gallons of jars with quarters, nickels, and dimes that he kept stored down in our seller. He said he would cash all those coins one day if he ever needed the money. It was years before he cashed all that money and that was quite an interesting story he shared with me some time later.

Many years later, Dad decided to cash in all those coins at the bank. When the Head Clerk of the bank saw all of the coins, he refused to cash them. Well, my dad said to him, "Since you will not take all my coins, I want to close all my accounts with your bank, right now!" Then my dad stood waiting for his funds to be given to him. My dad knew he had been with this bank for years and that he had plenty of savings in his account. Then Dad looked at me and said, "I also know, the bank uses my money to make more money for their bank, and now they have an issue of counting my coins. Well, I can take my money to another bank so I told them to close all my accounts." Then the Head Clerk told him to have a seat as he disappeared to another office. I'm sure he knew closing my dad's accounts was a big disadvantage to the bank, so, when the clerk returned, he apologized to him stating he made an error and they would cash the many coins and deposit them into his account. We stayed and waited, knowing they had machines to count coins and he needed to know how much money was deposited. Well, all I can say is that it was hundreds of dollars deposited and we smiled as we left the bank. My dad looked at me and said, "I understand how to manage my money and that's what I say to you, manage your money or it will manage you." I stood there feeling so proud of my dad who always taught me a good lesson. Yes, my Dad was a smart man and I admired him and wanted to be wise just like he was and I did.

FUN TIMES WITH FRIENDS

W hen I grew older in my teens, I continued to enjoy living on New Street because we had a variety of friends, most people got along, our physical needs were met, we had God-fearing parents who loved us, and to me," Life was Good."

My parents often allowed us to have a sleepover with our girlfriends for special occasions like our birthday or something. For this one particular sleepover, we decided to feature our favorite singing group, "Diana Ross and the Supremes" back in the 1960s. I was to be Diana Ross, Arlene and Joann were the Supremes. We all dressed in white and pink 2-piece silk night pajamas and we lip-synced the song and had our dance steps right on time. Everyone screamed and I mean it was a blast as we all pretended to be the Supremes. That was one memory that will always bring me joy and laughter at the good times all of us girls enjoyed while growing up.

AT THE SUPPER TABLE

Each weekday the Quinton Fire whistle blew and everyone in town heard that loud whistle and knew it was 5 p.m. It did not matter where we were, we had to run home because it was supper time and family time. Supper time was family time and I loved to eat so I was always on time. Also, I learned lots of things at the supper table about our family, our church, and life. All of us sat at the long wooden table together. My dad sat at the head of the table and my mom at the other end, the boys were on one side of the table and the girls sat on the other side. Mom was a great cook and supper time was everybody's favorite time, especially me. My dad always blessed the food and we all ate together. Dad always cut the meat first while sitting at the table. Dad had big hands and I would often think how strong he was and how he was always home on time.

After eating Dad always shared some words of wisdom with us like:

- I want all of you children to get a good education.
- We expect you to graduate and find a good job.
- Learn as much as you can, and always do your best.
- Always give the man a fair honest day's work and be on time.

- Don't ever be jealous of others.

- Be honest and respect others and remember:

- God bless the child who has his own. Get your own!

My Dad often talked to us at the supper table about the importance of God, family, and others. Dad worked hard managed his money and prioritized his needs because he said he wanted to earn his own since no one had to do anything for him. He said working for your own money makes you feel like a man or a woman with worth and value. Dad said it makes you feel good to know you contribute to society in some way. Being honest makes you trustworthy and others see and trust you. Having integrity helps to build your faith knowing you please God and others.

Dad said depending on others when you can earn your own money makes you vulnerable at times and sometimes, people will take advantage of you or they may devalue you because they know you have to depend on them.

While we were all still at the table, he would open our Report Cards and say, "Before I look at the grades, I'm going to read about your Behavior because you must behave well to learn and get good grades." If the behavior was good we smiled but if it was poor behavior we lowered our heads in shame. Dad would also tell us, "Children, never be jealous of what others have, all you have to do is work hard and manage your money and you can buy anything you want. Now be wise in your asking God for things. Everything is not for you to get."

Then Dad would turn and look straight at us girls and say, "I mean you girls too! Never depend on others to give you anything." I always had a feeling of being strong, smart, and secure as I sat at the table with my family because everything my dad said, he meant and did. When I looked at all my dad achieved with only an 8th grade education he was proof of what he said trusting God using wisdom and learning all you can to survive in this world. Especially since:

All of us children had daily chores to do each day and more on the weekends: Mom & Naomi always prepared the food during the week and baked cakes, pies, and cookies, and donuts on the weekend. Joann & I would clean the living and dining rooms and set the table. And Major & Carl washed the dishes, cleaned the cars, and cleaned the yard work.

Dad said he wanted us children to have educational advantages that he never had. That is why Dad talked about education so much that we had it in our minds to pursue as much schooling or training in any trade that would give us the opportunity in life that Dad felt he was denied. Then Dad went on to say, "I want you children to think for yourself! Don't follow the crowd because sometimes the crowd is wrong. If your friend wanted to jump off the Delaware Bridge, would you jump off too?" Dad looked at each of us to respond, "No." Dad then replied, "Children, you got to do what is right for yourself, each of you will have to deal with your choices in life!" Those words fell deep down in our hearts and minds. Dad was sure to plant a seed in our minds to not do wrong or disrespect our family.

I noticed that Dad and Mom often sat in the Living room talking and reading the Salem News Paper after supper time or just sitting and sharing their day. I always hoped I would have a husband who would sit and talk nicely together like my mom and dad. To me being kind to each other was a form of love. The Bible says married folks are to treat their spouse the way they want to be treated. I know God blesses us when we treat our spouse with love so I knew God was blessing my parents. I was thankful.

Dad stood tall at 6ft. 4 inches with jet black hair, and smooth brown skin, and was very handsome, he spoke with authority and wisdom. Dad never drank liquor, smoked cigarettes, fussed, and fought with others, and never cussed nor spoke foolishly. None of that talk was allowed in our house. Dad was honest and fair in his dealings. That is probably why folks called my dad when there was a family dispute.

HOME LIFE ON NEW STREET

My parents were married on June 14, 1939, and both my parents, Eugene, and Ruth, were adopted and neither of them had any siblings. They sometimes shared memories of their yearning for their natural parents during their childhood years. They both attended Quinton Elementary School where my mom completed the 6th grade and my Dad completed the 8th grade. This was all the schooling required for them in those days. However, my dad always regretted not completing the 12th grade because he knew the importance of education and was determined to learn all he could to provide for his family. He often inspired us to learn as much as possible in school.

In those days each house had a mom and a dad that worked to support the family. Seldom there were single mothers and children only. Even television shows had married couples with children like the Ozzie and Harriet Show, Father Knows Best, and the Donna Reed Show. These were models of how life was in those times. It was a time when married couples were what was considered good and respectable living.

On New Street, many of the wives stayed home with the 5 to 10 children in the family. Other wives stayed home to raise the family as Black women seldom worked outside the home unless they were doing washing and ironing for White people to help with their income. Blacks often had low-paying jobs due to their lack of skills, education, and other restrictions. But we were blessed by the Lord with a garden, chickens, fishing, hunting, going to the tomatoes or bean fields, sewing, making our own clothes, sharing homemade health cures, along with a lot of friends, and dancing to the latest songs and sharing happy memories with families and friends. We always found ways to make the best of bad situations.

Our street only had one White family that lived on New Street and that was Teddy and Albee Nickles family that lived two houses from us. We treated them just like they were Black folks and Teddy was my brother Carl's best friend. They became Boy Scouts together and neither was treated any differently from the rest of the families on our street. We had fun and little did I know how much it helped us to resolve our differences and later laugh together as we learned to exchange other points of view. Our family and many others shared and learned from each other and that helped us mature. I loved that because I always wanted to learn and enjoy my relationships.

DANCING AND PRANCING

However, there was a particular family that lived right next to our house who caused all kinds of discord in our neighborhood and cussed and was a troublemaker. And then there was another woman with 8 children who moved down the street. This lady had a Juke Box in her house and when people found out about it, everyone was at her house dancing, putting money in the Juke Box, and dancing the night away. It was so loud you could hear it down the street! When my Mom found out we were down there, she told us she was going to tell Dad if we ever went down there again! I asked Mom, "What was wrong when everyone was just dancing?" Mom said, "You may not understand but a whole lot of trouble can come to dancing and having all kinds of people come to have fun at your house with all the boys, girls, and men." Later, I heard they were drinking, smoking and some Hanky Panky was going on. Well, I did not understand at first but a whole lot of trouble started after that and I heard some things I am glad I was not included. Yes, Mom and Dad were right as usual. So I listened when they told me to think for myself and be conscious of my surroundings.

Dad always warned us to stay away from trouble and fights

so when he told us we knew to do as he said. On Saturdays, Dad allowed us to go to the Movie Theater in Salem. It cost only 50 cents to pay a man named Bear who collected our money to go to the Balcony. All the Blacks had to sit in the balcony while the Whites sat downstairs in the best seats. It never bothered me because it was cheaper to be seated on the balcony. A lot of the Blacks and I never realized it was segregation until years later.

Then there was a place called the Blue Bird, which was a food counter and dance club in which we had to pay a small fee of 25 cents where we could dance to the tunes of Aretha Franklin, Mary Wells, and Marvin Gaye to name a few. It was very orderly and the older Black couple would keep an eye on everyone to ensure there were no problems among us. Dad always said before we left home on Saturday night, "Girls, you all stick together! Don't leave each other alone and be home by midnight!" And lastly, he said, "Be careful!" We were sure to follow Dad's instructions because Dad did not play!

When the Blue Bird closed, the Ice House opened up to dance and play tunes on the Juke Box. They called it the Ice House Juke Joint for us teens to dance. I got to learn some new dances and new friends.

During those times there were names for the different dances like the Twist, the Stroll, the Crossfire, the Slop, the Mashed Potatoes, and the Bop. We had a great time learning the steps to the latest dances. Those were good memories too.

FIGHTS AND DISCORDS ON NEW STREET

There were some fights on New Street during those days, but it was mostly "Fair Fights." Most times fights started when someone knocked a stick off the other person's shoulder, then the fight was on! Fair fights were always one-on-one and a crowd to watch the fight.

There was an incident when a neighbor was attacking one of my sisters and that girl had the nerve to even run into our kitchen to attack and fight my sister! But when my Dad found out what happened, that was the last draw for him!

Well, my Dad said, "I am sick and tired of how their family disrespects me and my children, and other families on this street." My Dad told my sister to get dressed and go outside and fight that girl because we had had enough of their family harassing the neighborhood and we were not taking anymore!

The fight was on and my sister fought that girl fair and square! The entire street crowded around and watched my sister standing boldly as she fought that girl in the street. Even a carload of folks stopped to watch the fight. There was no bloodshed, but the hair was pulled out, punches were landed, clothes were torn off of the other girl and everything was exposed! All the young boys went crazy in seeing all that going on. Everyone on the street talked about that fight for weeks! That girl's mother and family were so angry and humiliated! But from that time on their family never bothered our family again. Everyone on our street talked about that fight for days and was glad my dad allowed her to stand up for herself.

I was shocked when my dad told my sister to go out there and fight that girl because he was always a peaceful man! But I see how important it is when others disrespect you and your children and then you realize it's time to put a stop to it all! I was so proud of my sister too. She did not know it, but she stood for the whole neighborhood in stopping that trouble-making family from harassing and disrespecting us.

We all walked with pride after that episode and never had any problem thereafter. No one called the Police and the fight was resolved and everyone eventually went back to being friends. This was how folks on New Street dealt with each other.

PARENTS WORKING HARD ON NEW STREET

Besides disputes, I also noticed that many parents sacrificed and worked many jobs to raise their families. I recalled there were a lot of folks working all kinds of jobs to make ends meet. There was the Rag Man, the Ice Man, the Fish Man, the Bread Man, the Milk Man, the Fruit Man, the Number's Man, the Snapper Turtle Man, and others who would come to your house to sell items.

There was a family that lived three doors from our house. The entire family would get up early in the morning and go to the bean fields or tomato fields because that was the only means of income. That family had three teenage boys, a set of twin girls, and two older sisters, and the family went to the fields along with both the Father and Mother every day of the week but Sunday.

Sundays were always different from any other day. Even at our house, we were to keep Sunday Holy and go to church. There was no playing cards, listening to Rock and Roll, dancing, or going to a movie, and some of the mothers even cooked on Saturday because Sunday was a day of rest. Almost all the stores were closed in respect of Sunday. It was not unusual for no one to work on Sunday. During those times people had respect for resting on the Sabbath Day.

But just like clockwork on Monday, I watched them go to the fields early in the morning and later that day they would return home from the field, and they always went straight into their house and seldom came out to play. I realized working in the hot sun all day and picking beans and/or tomatoes was very hard work. I was sure that they were extremely tired because they worked in the steaming hot sun in the field so they needed plenty of rest for the next day.

My heart felt sorrow for them because they were a very nice family and so I was especially kind to them. I also prayed for them at night to get a better job to make a living. I also empathized with them because when I went to the bean field years ago the sun was so hot and the work was so hard, that I decided would never work a job that hard to make a living. I made up my mind, right then that I was going to get my education just like my Dad said over and over again at the supper table. My Dad always shared stories to make us think. One of his favorite questions to make us think was: "If your friend jumped off the Delaware Memorial Bridge, would you jump too?" Of course, we said, "No." Then he said, "That's right, you must think for yourself and don't just do what others do, you must think of the consequences. So, you need to be wise and think for yourself and get your education. Education will open up doors for you to make a living and not have to scrape for pennies or break your back to survive." I knew my Dad was right. That's why I worked hard in school and prayed to the Lord to help me learn and become a teacher to help other children make a good living.

When I look back now, I realize that New Street was a good place for me to learn new things, mature, and grow up in a very safe and healthy environment.

MY PARENTS

My parents, Rev. Eugene Henry Cheak and Ruth Brown Cheak were married on June 14, 1939, in our house at 146 New Street, Quinton, NJ. They also raised all seven of us children together in that house and we lived there all our lives. My parents attended Quinton Elementary School. My Dad completed the 8th grade which was all that was required for foster children during those times. Dad had no sisters or brothers and was placed in an orphanage as a foster child moving from family to family until his later years. Often my Dad spoke of his regret for not knowing any of his family and that is why I thought he often read the Bible and trusted on God for his needs. Dad was also disappointed not to be permitted to graduate from the 12th grade. However, he made it clear he loved his family and wanted the best for them. He also knew the advantages of education and he wanted his children to have the opportunities he was denied. Dad continually encouraged us to learn as much as possible in getting a trade or education of some kind. Dad said he was determined to accomplish his aspirations in life regardless of being deprived of formal education. Dad inspired me to achieve my heart's desire as he shared portions of his life with us.

Now, I want to tell you a little about my father's early childhood and how great and wonderful our Savior is as He guides and protects us in this big, beautiful, and mixed-up world we live in. My father shared this story with me and I know it is important for you to know this:

Eugene Henry Cheak was born never knowing his father who died months before he was born and he never knew his mother because she died shortly after his birth. Eugene was not only a parentless child in this great big, lonely world but imagine having neither parent as a newborn to love you and care for you and not even having any brothers or sisters to hold on to and love as you grow up. I found that to be a lonely life as a young child.

Parents are special people who always have much love for their children. Most of us are blessed to have at least one natural parent or sibling to love and care for us, yet Eugene was put in an orphanage as a child of the State. Later he was moved into three foster homes during his childhood. He said he felt unloved and there was always plenty of work to be done as most families needed boys to work the farms as free labor for them. But in the midst of it all, God was with him. Eugene went to church and often listened to the preacher who said, "We can trust and depend on God for all our needs. We must surrender our lives to the

Lord!" Eugene believed what the Bible said so Eugene began to pray to God for a better life with love and a family. Eugene prayed often and drew close to God for his needs and God has blessed him with a family of his own, friends, health, a good job, and a church family and blessings every day.

This story is to encourage and draw you closer to our Lord as it did me. For if parents live and teach their children to love God, others, and themselves the blessings will follow. Yes, all of us will go through the ups and downs of life. But we can depend on God to give us wisdom, strength, and favor as we follow Him.

Eugene had only one relative which was Uncle Johnathan, his mother's only brother and now he could hardly provide for himself so finally his uncle had no other choice than to place Eugene in the Good Samaritan Orphanage, in Newark, NJ.

My father said he remembered how cold, empty, lonely, and sad a place it was to live. He recalled how they often fed them water and rye bread. My father said even now he cannot stand the smell of rye bread as it brings back such sad dark memories.

But God was with Eugene as He opened a door in the Adams family in Shiloh, NJ, who were Christians. God placed him on the Adams' farm with three other young Adams boys who knew the Lord too. Eugene finally felt the love of a family at Mommy

Adams's home. The three brothers made him feel like he belonged to their family. God smiled on Eugene because He had plans for him to be a servant.

God took him through many trials on his journey which made Eugene realize that he could only depend on God which increased his faith and endurance to serve the Lord. That is how Eugene became a strong Soldier in the Army of God.

He eventually married Ruth and began their family, He knew he could depend on God for all his needs.

My father and mother's example taught us children to live, serve, and depend on God for all our needs. God cannot fail.

My parents, Rev. Eugene Henry Cheak and Ruth Brown Cheak were Christians and they were serious about living out our faith in an everyday way of life. We all attended Sunday School and church each week. This was my favorite time as I loved Sunday School, church picnics, youth fellowships, and learning that God is always right and wants the best for us. I learned to pray often and always felt God's protection as my faith developed. Those early teachings strengthened my spiritual growth throughout my life journey. I loved our family and I thanked God for my wonderful parents.

My prayer and purpose are to share our family history with

my children, grandchildren, friends, and anyone who reads my story because our family heritage helps us know who we are and what we should know about ourselves to be passed on to future generations. This reveals the whys and where we get our beliefs, values, behaviors, who are our relatives, our strengths and gifts, and the many things about ourselves and our family members that make us who we are. These stories will give you value, worth, and strength as you grow into the person you are meant to be. These experiences need to be passed on to loved ones.

I am so proud that the Cheak Family has contributed to making a positive difference in this world by the way we lived and the God we served. May everyone who reads my story be inspired to share their story and to serve the King of Kings and Lord of Lords.

My Dad was a very handsome man as he stood 6 ft. 4 inches tall with thick black hair and smooth caramel skin with dark brown eyes. He walked with pride and had a voice of authority and wisdom. People often called him when there was a dispute because he was fair and non-violent and they trusted his judgments.

We were one of the first Black families to get a black and white television (TV) which I loved to watch and learn about other people in the world. TV was another world as I sat and learned so many things on TV that I never knew.

On Saturdays, my Dad loved watching wrestling on TV. I mean you better get out of the way when my dad would turn on wrestling. He would shout and say, "Get 'um, knock him down!" and he would get so excited I got excited too! It's so funny, my Dad loved seeing the wrestlers' tag team and he would stand and shout, "Knock him out!" as the wrestlers jumped on the rope and threw each other around in the ring. I believe, most people would be shocked to see my Dad so excited because he was not a violent man and always seemed so cool when dealing with most people. But Dad had me getting excited as he routed for his team. I loved watching wrestling with my Dad. Those were special moments of excitement.

Dad was also the first on New Street to buy a telephone. The phones were always black with long cords. We had to memorize our phone number which was 1 2 8 9 J 3. We would pick the phone up and tell the operator what number we wanted to call. But, we had a party line so when we sometimes picked up the phone we could hear the neighbors talking on the phone to other people. Sometimes people would quietly pick up the phone so you could not hear a click to let others know someone else picked up the line and listen to the party line and get in other people's business or listen to what they were gossiping about. Some folks even had big arguments and fights when they heard people talking about them. But we always hung up and waited until they finished before we could call out to anyone. Often the neighbors would come and ask if they could use our phone. We would always let them use our phone but we would tell them not to make a long-distance number because it cost us more money. Sometimes they would sneak and make long-distance calls so we stayed near to hear who they were dialing.

Another thing about Dad was he was always on time. My Dad always came straight home from work and was always right on time for supper, weddings, meetings, and any other commitments he made because he said it showed his integrity. Dad always spoke of being on time. He always made sure we had family fun like going to the Boardwalk in Atlantic City on Easter or having wonderful Christmas times together. We also had church socials at our house for our church fundraising along with picnics with our Church family. The Mummers Parade in Philadelphia was the yearly finale along with seeing our Grandpop Brown each year. Whatever plan was made, we all had to follow the plan. Dad said plans will work if you work your plan. I found we always had an enjoyable plan because we worked the plan.

My parents never cussed or fought with each other or anyone else, and no drinking or smoking went on in our house. Everyone had to go to church on Sundays and go to school, behave, and do their best. Both my parents loved the Lord and respected others and I was so glad. I liked the peacefulness and calmness in our home, so it was easy to follow their examples. I just saw it as a way of life that was fair and peaceful.

Throughout my life, my Mom had a quiet spirit and she had a lot of compassion and love as she took care of us. She stood 4 feet 9 inches tall with a small petite physique as she always had a smile for everyone. Mom worked at Uncle Bud's Laundry and later she did housework for the White folks on Main Street. Mom was very thoughtful and kind and she always had something nice to say. She would often say to us children, "If you don't have something nice to say about someone, don't say anything." That made me thoughtful about how important what we say matters. It also made me realize how unkind words impact others.

Mom and my sister, Naomi, were like two peas in a pot as they were always preparing dinner, cooking, or baking homemade cakes and pies. Everyone on New Street loved their delicious Ginger Cakes and Sugar Cakes! My Mom was also the

Church Communion Stewardess which was a very honorable position. She washed, ironed, and prepared the Communion Linen for our Holy Communion services at our church. Mom was well-liked and respected. My Dad often called her, "Girly" in an affectionate way. Mom always supported Dad like a king or best friend. They were good examples of what I expected marriage to be like. I often thanked God that she was my loving Mom.

One special memory of Mom was when she went to get her hair done at Ms. Greggs Salon in Salem. Mom always brought Joann and me a gift from the 5 and 10 Cent Stores. That day she bought me a book called, "*The Little Red Hen.*" I could not read well at that time, but as I read that book it came alive to me. "The Little Red Hen" was always baking and doing things for others. And we always said that Mom was our Little Red Hen and Mom always smiled whenever we called her our Little Red Hen.

Whenever Mom went to Salem, she would take either Joann or me with her because she could afford to take us one at a time. This particular time, Mom took me to the 5 and 10 Cent Store and she said I could pick out one toy for myself so I went looking for a toy. Suddenly, I turned and there stood a midget. I was shocked because I had never seen a real midget, I mean he was so tiny and shorter than me but he had the face of a grown man.

I could not take my eyes off of him! Then he tried to walk past me and I held out my arms to block him from passing because I was amazed at how strange he looked to me. But when my Mom saw me, she grabbed me and reprimanded me for bothering the little man. She told me to never tease people who are different and never bother them. I felt ashamed as she scolded me. She told me to find a toy so I began looking again, and suddenly, I looked down each aisle and my mom was gone. I began to cry as I went outside the store and walked down the street, fearing my mother left me for being bad to the midget. I sat on the curve crying as the fear of losing my mom pierced my heart. Then a lady came and asked me what was wrong and I told her as I sat thinking if my mom forgives me, I will never tease other people again. Then suddenly my mother came walking down the street toward me. What a wonderful feeling to see my mom as she held my hand and I tightly held her hand. I was so relieved to see her as I learned a very important lesson that day. I never teased others again as I remember the lesson I learned. I felt the consequences of my misbehaving with the midget. That experience impacted me in wanting to do the right thing whenever my parents or those in charge instructed me. From that time on I hated to get in trouble for not following the rules.

As little children, when family or friends came to our house and sat talking around the table Joann and I would sit under the big wooden table as the adults talked because we liked to hear grownups talking about all kinds of things, so we sat quietly to listen. But when we would hear someone say, "Little Pitchers have Big Ears." Often, I would look at Joann wondering what those words meant. Suddenly, one of the adults would look under the table and say, "You young children go outside and play!" We then hurried outside. It took me some time before I understood that Little Pitchers were the two of us who they were referring to.

BROTHERS AND SISTERS

While growing up, I always loved to learn and understand life. I watched my family, especially my older siblings. I noticed that the first three siblings in our family were called by their middle name, not their first name like the rest of us. My oldest brother, Eugene Major Cheak was named after our Dad, but we called him Major. He always had close friends and he loved to have a good time dancing and showing off, he was fast with his hands and bragged about how good he could fight. Major was very popular with the ladies and was good-looking too. In his late teens, he went to Atlantic City, found a job, and soon fell in love and married sweet and beautiful Tina. They had children so later Major asked me to babysit for them in the summer. I was so happy to go away from home for the summer, but I was shocked that I got so homesick and my heart actually ached and I cried myself to sleep each night for the entire month. I was so glad to return home to my family!

Years later, when both Joann and I headed for Atlantic City to stay with our oldest brother, whom people called, "Cheek-o" and not Major. He was very popular and let us both stay and work in the summer to earn money for the school year. So we both got waitress jobs and saved our money to buy school clothes and other needs. We both loved Atlantic City and all the excitement as we walked on the crowded streets of Kentucky Avenue where Club Harlem was the main attraction for the upcoming stars. We had great times and each summer we looked forward to working in A.C.

Then came my second brother, Joseph Carl Cheak. Carl was very smart, ambitious, and adventurous. He joined the Boy Scouts along with his best friend, Teddy. We were all so proud of them in their uniforms. As a scout, Carl first built a chicken coup in the backyard where he raised small hens. Then he showed me how to collect the eggs and taught me how to fry eggs six different ways. I was amazed at what I learned! Both Carl and Teddy soon built a large brick fireplace in our backyard. At night we roasted marshmallows and hot dogs with our friends. It was so much fun! Often, they would go fishing or crabbing down at the wharf and we all sit out back eating the delicious fresh fish along with those tasty crabs as we ate and joked about all kinds of things with family and friends. I enjoyed listening and learning about others. That was always a special time for socializing with friends.

One particular day Carl asked me if I knew how to tell time

and I said, "No." He then found an old alarm clock and taught me how to tell time. I felt so good as I learned and understood how to tell time. That experience built my confidence too! Carl also loved sports and Carl was the first to introduce me to Cashes Clay who later changed his name to Muhammed Ali. Carl predicted that one day Muhammed Ali would be the *Heavy Weight Champion of the World*! Not only did he achieve the Title 1 time but *three times - Muhammed Ali became "The Heavy Weight Champion of the World!"*

My brother knew what he was talking about as he saw how great a boxer Muhammed Ali was from the onset! Even to this day, I think of Carl every time Muhammed Ali is mentioned. Yes, I do believe that Muhammad Ali not only changed the game of boxing, but Muhammed Ali was the greatest boxer to me! And Carl was the Greatest Brother to me.

Years later, Carl joined the U.S. Air Force and traveled all over the world and I constantly wrote him letters. Later he came home and married his sweetheart, Geneva Brown (AKA: Jill) I recalled, that Jill was the only girl Carl ever brought home to meet the family. Carl completed his 8 years of service to return to civilian life. Later, they had a son. I would often stay over at their house and go to parties with them. These were special times.

My sister, Ruth Naomi Cheak was four years older than me. Naomi was always at mom's side in the kitchen. Even as a child, I remembered Naomi (Nay) and Mom pretending to bake and have tea parties. When Naomi grew up, she loved to bake, cook, and find new recipes to serve the family. On Saturday they stayed in the kitchen making homemade cakes, rolls, donuts, cookies, and those delicious ginger cakes and sugar cakes that the whole neighborhood bought and loved to eat.

Naomi, Mary, and Leona were older teenage girls that I admired as they dressed and acted like young ladies as they went to school. I wanted to be like them. At night, Naomi would let me roll her curly hair and I felt special as we talked together. She was always very honest. I recall once I asked her about babies being born and she told me the truth, I was so shocked. I could not believe it at first, but she was telling me the truth. I was amazed!

One day, Carl brought a friend home named William Graves. Nay liked him but he soon joined the Navy. They fell in love with each other and Nay wrote him every other day. She was so happy as she sometimes read the letters to me. They sounded so "in love" I blushed to even read that mushy stuff. And as soon as he completed the Navy, he married Naomi and I was her Maid of

Honor. In time they had 5 children. She became a Head Start Teacher, and later she advanced to a Day Care Director.

Nay encouraged me to apply for the teacher position at Head Start where she worked. I got the job and then we found my first house in Delaware a block away. I looked up to Nay and to me, she was my biggest fan always encouraging me to move forward. Naomi was honest, faithful, and strong, and just like Mom she always loved to help others. She was strong in her faith too. When she believed something, she would stand alone on her belief in God.

Eventually, we lived right around the corner from each other. I would often stop by her house right after work. We talked and enjoyed so many things together. Throughout life, we stayed close and planned lots of trips for the family. And we often said we continued what Mom and Dad would do to be sure the family had good times together.

As years passed, Dad went to glory and later Mom moved in with Nay at the age of 88. Nay took Mom to the Senior Center where she worked as a day care director. Each day Nay would pick Mom up after work. Nay and I planned trips to Virginia Beach, NY Ski Trips, and Williamsburg to ensure we all had a good time. No matter if it was our family vacations, retreats, or church we would push Mom in the wheelchair and away we all went. We never left Mom out because we always had Mom recite one of her poems even at the age of 94. Naomi was so caring about the family and she loved the Lord.

About 14 months after I was born, my sister, Joann arrived. We looked so much alike that folks thought we were twins. To tell us apart, Mom dressed us alike with Joann in red and me in blue. JoAnn was always by my side and we were very close but different personalities. JoAnn only talked, if I did until she got older and she talked a lot more than me. Joann knew a lot of people and sometimes she got into arguments and even fights but I wouldn't allow anyone to hurt her. I was a thinker and loved making smart decisions. I started school a year before her but I shared at Show and Tell Class that I had Impetigo. Soon after, the school principal called me into the hallway and told me not to return until I was rid of the contagious disease. I cried all the way home and I ended up staying home for a whole year! I stayed home for the school year and later Joann and I started school together. Everyone still thought we were twins.

For more than 8 or 9 years, Joann was the youngest child, then Mom announced she was having a baby! We were all so excited to welcome a baby to our family. Finally, one day as Joann and I were on our steps playing Jack's, suddenly Dad and Mom drove up in the car, and when Mom stepped out of the car she held the most beautiful baby girl I had ever seen! Our new baby sister's name was Rose! She was wrapped in a beautiful soft pink blanket and Mom had a soft pastel green coat on that simply looked elegant as she stepped out of the car. We all fussed over Rose, she was such a joy! Rose was the perfect name for her as she was such a sweet adorable baby. It was a shift of position for Joann as Rose came on the scene. I noticed that Joann realized that someone else was taking the "Baby" position. I can imagine 8 or 9 years is a long time to hold that position as "Baby" when someone like Rose suddenly comes to instantly take her place. Soon the reality was accepted and we all pampered our baby sister Rose.

I noticed as Rose grew up, she loved candy and she always found ways to get someone to treat her with a bar of candy. Rose was lovable, quiet, and easygoing. She would often help me do things around the house. Rose was very close to Mom and the three oldest children were on their way out on their own when Rose was growing up. So Rose was raised as an only child when all of us older children were moving out on our own.

Then three years after Rose arrived, our little brother, Michael

Cornell Cheak was born. We were so happy to have a little brother. I found boys were very different from girls, but I like learning how boys behave and I found that Michael was so smart and very active. As a young boy, he jumped and played with a lot of energy. He knew all our names and pronounced words clearly and I could tell he was going to be smart like my brother, Carl. Michael was the 7th child which was the last one in our family.

CHURCH AND OUR FAITH

I remember us children walking two miles to the church early on Sunday mornings. Dad made sure we knew how important it was to serve God. Later, Dad bought a car and we rode to church as a family. My parents always sat on the left side and the fifth pew with Mom, Joann, and I next to him. Church always seemed so long, but seeing the folks dressed up in lovely hats and outfits was beautiful.

The preacher was often excited and people said, "Amen" as he preached. I thought that was exciting as I listened to the preacher talking about God and how He made the world and could see everything we did and thought according to the Bible. That made me think about so many things.

My Dad was well known in all the churches for singing familiar hymns like Amazing Grace, The Old Rugged Cross, and Jesus Keep Me Near the Cross or one of my favorite hymns was, When I Wake Up in Glory or I Know It Was the Blood. I often traveled with my Dad when he had to sing at other churches. I loved visiting other churches and I loved the way he sang with such feeling and sincerity.

I remember there was always some kind of church trip going on. Sometimes it would be the church picnics at Willow Grove

Park. During that time Dad was the Sunday School Superintendent so we were sure to go. Because we had very little money we would pack a lunch and picnic tables would be assigned to our group. Dad would buy the group tickets and distribute them to all of us. I remember I would go on all kinds of rides, especially the bumping cars. I was afraid to ride the Roller Coaster and the other wild rides because they made me sick, but I loved watching others ride as they screamed and waved their hands to the onlookers. Often, I ran out of tickets and I recall my Dad, coming over to me and asking me what was wrong. I told him I used up all my tickets. He looked at me, reached into the large envelope in his hand, and gave me a hold page of tickets. I was so happy as I ran into the park to enjoy more rides. Those were fun times with our church family and friends that brought me good memories. Our church always had something for us children to enjoy and grow our faith to feel a part of the church. Going to church was always a place I looked forward to going.

Dad was a leader at Haven Methodist Church and he was the Sunday School Superintendent and various times he was a delegate at the Delaware Methodist Conference. Often, he assisted the Pastors that were assigned to our church and many times he sat in the pulpit with other ministers. Dad loved the Lord and he was serious and very committed to living the Christian life. That is why we were not surprised he became our local church minister.

He also loved learning and he loved books, especially the Bible. We had large bookcases filled with all kinds of Bible stories, encyclopedias, and an array of Mother Goose books to read. Dad encouraged us to read and learn things.

All of us had to go to Sunday School and Church which was where I learned to trust God. I learned about stories and scriptures in the Bible and how to live according to the Word of God. Church was a special and good place to go.

Early one Sunday morning Dad would sit in the Living Room and read the large Bible and just sit quietly. I crawled on the floor so he could not see me. I lay on the floor waiting to hear him read, but he just sat quietly. Suddenly, I popped up from the side of the couch and asked Dad, "What are you doing sitting so still? He looked at me in surprise and said, "I'm meditating on the Word of God and listening to what the Bible is saying to me." I said, "Oh" and thought about what he said and I learned for myself, how important it is to meditate on the Word to learn the true meaning of what the Word is saying to me when I read it. I still do that today and have learned many things in a much deeper way.

I listened to Rev. John as he jumped up and talked about the Holy Spirit. I watched him and I wanted the Holy Spirit too. I loved to hear the Word of God. I remember when I was in Church and I accepted Christ as my Savior when I was 12 years old. I was so glad about it! However, I felt that Jesus was already my friend as I met Him years ago as I sat in our church listening to the preacher and going to Sunday school learning all about the Bible and how Christ died for us all.

Years later my father became a local Pastor at our church. Then he was asked to Pastor at Bethany Christian Church in Bridgeton NJ. Bethany Church needed a pastor for a year while deciding how to move forward. Surprisingly he remained the Pastor at Bethany for 14 years. My Dad agreed to Pastor Bethany but also, decided he would remain at our Home Church. My sister, Naomi would drive them faithfully each Sunday to both churches as Mom and Dad were much older than them.

One day Naomi asked me to drive Mom and Dad to church as she was unable to take them this particular Sunday. I was glad to drive my parents to church for her. That Sunday as I drove out of the church parking lot, a large junk truck was in front of me that was going very slow as we road down Route 49. Well, as we road for miles, the junk on the truck was so wide and so high, that I was unable to see clearly to safely pass the truck. I tried several times but each time another car was coming and I had to reduce my speed and wait for the next safe change.

As we slowly followed the truck, suddenly, the driver of the truck waved his hand to me telling me the way was safe to pass him. So I sped up and began passing the junk truck and suddenly a car came over the hill and was coming directly towards me, I held on tight to the steering wheel as the car facing me came right at us. The truck was on my right side with no place for me to avoid a car crash! Suddenly and unexpectedly, our car was turned around and sitting on the shoulder of the road and we had avoided a terrible accident. Shocked! Was how we all felt as we looked at each other saying, "What Happened?" As we sat in our car knowing we did not turn around, nor did we hit the other car, which was moving in the direction of home instead of toward Bridgeton. There was something supernatural about it all because, one minute the car and we were about to have a head-on collision, and the next minute we were safe on the shoulder of the road. To me, it was a miracle and I know it was God sending His angels to protect us! All I could do was thank God for His protection because no one but God could have lifted our car to safety! I know that God is real and what a Great God we serve.

CHRISTMAS AT OUR HOUSE

Christmas was our favorite time of the year and all our family could not wait until Christmas day. But one thing for sure, Mom and Dad always reminded us it was Christ's Birthday and they made sure we did not forget that. Mom and Dad had a special way of celebrating Christmas each year. I loved it and that is the same way I celebrate Christmas at our house, even to this day! And this is what they did:

- We all went to bed early and laid out our clothes to dress in the morning.

- Then my parents locked the bedroom doors to keep up from sneaking up.

- Breakfast was brought to us in the morning and we ate in our bedroom.

- Once all 7 children of us were ready, we had to line up with the youngest children first and we had to SING all together: JOY TO THE WORLD as we walked down the stairs and completed the first stanza before we ran to look under the tree to see what gifts we got.

- Mom and Dad always had a Christmas Tree for themselves separate from us children in the living room. All of the best candy and decorations were there after the grand excitement was over in the dining room with all of us kids. I was never disappointed at Christmas time. It was always the best day ever!

- Later in the afternoon Mom would cook a big turkey or ham and the older children who were adults came over to feast with dinner and then we all exchanged gifts with each other. It was such a wonderful time with the family.

One of the reasons my parents made Christmas so special to us was that on Christmas Eve nothing in our home was decorated for Christmas because there was no Christmas tree, gifts, candy, lights, or anything in view at our house. But Mom and Dad made sure we were all sound to sleep on Christmas Eve as our parents put up the Christmas tree, decorated it, and put all the gifts they had kept hidden from us children were then put under the fully decorated Christmas tree, along with bowls of fresh fruit, all kinds of candy in colorful candy dishes and every gift wrapped and marked for each individual.

Then early Christmas morning we all had to get dressed, and line up to sing "Joy to the World." We marched down the stairs and stood with wide eyes open as we had to finish the song. Then we ran to see what gifts were under the Christmas tree for us! It was an exciting time. It felt like a "Miraculous Christmas" morning as we all celebrated at our house! It was wonderful and we all were so happy about our special celebration at our house every Christmas!

Also, Mom and Dad always had a small special tree decorated in the front room with their special gifts to each other and gifts we also gave them. They also had the best assorted candies and fruit on display as the front room was their special place. I thought that it was so sweet of them to have their own tree together because that showed how special they were to each other. I have so many fond memories of my childhood at Christmas time that I knew I would continue when I grew up and had my own family someday.

Then the following week we all looked forward to our family trip to the Mummers Parade and to visit our Grandpop Brown. It was always a favorite time for our family!

THE NEW YEAR PARADE

One of the trips throughout our family was the New Year's Parade in Philadelphia. PA. I remember our family watching the Philadelphia New Year's Parade on TV early in my life when I was about 5 or 6 years old. There was one time I heard my Dad say, "Let's go to the New Year's Parade, in Philadelphia!" I got so excited at the thought of seeing the parade live with all those people on TV. Now whenever my Dad said something, he did exactly what he said. So I knew, we were going to the Mummers Parade!!!

When it was close to the New Year, Dad and Mom would tell us the plan. First, we were to pack a large lunch to last all day. Then were had to make cartons of hot tea, and hot chocolate and be sure to have fruit, potato chips, and some candy. Now, Mom and us girls prepared the food at night, so we were all ready to put the food in the car in the morning. Dad would gas up the car the day before to prevent any delays in arrival. We all had to go to bed extra early and our clothes were laid out the night before so there would be no delays. Our clocks were set to leave at 5:00 a.m.

When Mom woke us up at 4:00 a.m., it seemed like nighttime because it was so dark. But we all got up, put on our clothes, and placed the food and other items in the car. Dad knew the way and he especially went early so that we could get the same parking place each year like clockwork. The corner of Broad and South Street was perfect to sit along the streets as we watched the Mummers Parade. They danced, sang, and strut straight down Broad Street. They wore multi-colored costumes and floats that took all year to prepare. It was so beautiful, I felt like I was in a dream as I watched the parade in person. I loved and looked forward to our family trip every year! Yes, Dad and Mom always made sure we had wonderful memories.

VISITING GRANDPOP BROWN

In addition to going to the New Year's Parade, we visited my mother's real father. My mother was told about him after she was adopted by the Berry family. She was very happy that her father finally found her so she would visit him sometimes.

The second reason was the location when we started going to the New Year's Parade. My Dad would leave early for Philadelphia so he could park on the corner of Broad and South Street which was the same block Grandpop Brown lived. Whenever it was really cold standing out there watching the Mummers, we decided to go visit Grandpop in his warm apartment. Grandpop Brown lived four blocks down on South Street in an old apartment house.

When we rang the doorbell, Grandpop would stick his head out the third-floor window to see who it was. Then he would buzz us into the building. We had to walk up three long flights of stairs. Grandpop would have his lady friend, Ms. Marge, open the door. Sometimes when we would arrive Grandpop's friends would be sitting at the table drinking alcohol.

My mother had told us before the trip that Grandpop had a

"Speak Easy." I asked, "What's a Speak Easy?" Mom told us Grandpop sold unlicensed liquor after hours. People spoke easily so others would not get him into trouble. I whispered, OK but that sounded strange to me. Grandpop was very old but he had a nice smile and he moved very slowly. His lady friend Marge was also very old and she was often sick when we went to visit. My Mom would sit next to her father and I could see she favored him. They both smiled and I could tell they were happy to see us.

Later as the years progressed while at the New Year's Parade, we would go to the huge movie theater on South Street. It cost 50 cents to watch as many movies as possible that were playing that day. The movie was different from the one in our little town of Salem, NJ. In Salem, the movie theater was large downstairs for the White children to sit and watch the movie but all of the Black children had to sit on the small balcony. It cost 50 cents for one movie. But in Philadelphia, everyone sat together in the large theater and watched two or three movies together.

When we returned home from seeing the Mummers, we told all our friends how exciting it was to see the beautiful costumes, dancers, clowns, floats, and celebrities. We also shared that we went to a large movie theater where we all sat together to watch two or three movies one after the other.

Visiting a large city like Philadelphia made me realize how big and different the world is and that enriched my thinking in the way I saw the world. I loved the fact that Dad and Mom took us to different places and helped us learn more about the way of the world.

I also bragged about the fact that we visited our Grandpop living in Philadelphia, PA. Then I whispered to them that our Grandpop had a "Speak Easy." I knew that none of the kids on our street ever heard of a "Speak Easy," so they asked us, "What is a Speak Easy and why are you whispering?" I told them that Grandpop sold unlicensed liquor after hours, so people had to "Speak Easy" so others would not hear them and get Grandpop in trouble. Then they smiled and said, "Wow, I did not know that!" I felt smart like my Dad as I smiled.

No other children on our street went on trips to the New Year's Parade as we did; that is probably the reason I always felt that we had a good and exciting life with our parents. They did a lot of energizing things with the family.

<u>RIDE OF FAITH</u>

Years later as I grew more mature I had an experience that made me know how real God truly is. That experience drew me closer to my faith in God. I thank God every time I think about it, for it could have gone another way. I might not have been here to share this experience. It happened like this:

One day my Mom and Joann came back from Salem and Mom not only got her hair done at the hairdresser, but she got Joann's hair done too. Joann's hair looked so pretty and shiny with the beautiful waves and high Shirley Temple curls laid at the side of her face. Joann's hair looked so pretty and my hair was so dull and nappy. I begged Mom to take me to get my hair done too. Mom said, "Maybe the next time, Diane. I don't have enough money for now." Weeks later, I asked Mom about taking me to Salem and getting my hair done, but she said she didn't have enough money yet. Then I asked her if I could catch the bus by myself and go to Salem and get a few other items for myself. I convinced Mom I was old enough to catch the bus and return home, after all, I was 14 years old. Mom agreed to give me 10 cents for the bus and some money to buy a few items. I felt so proud of myself as I stood on Main Street, in Quinton waiting for the bus.

As I stood waiting for the bus, cars passed by the highway and it seemed like the bus was running late. But I waited on that corner, feeling anxious to get to Salem when suddenly, a large black car stopped right in front of me. I looked and saw a big, fat, White man winding his car window down and asked me, "Little girl, do you want a ride to Salem?" I looked at him, and then I looked at the 10 cents for the bus that Mom gave me. I thought to myself, *"10 cents would be mine to spend,"* so I hopped in the man's car and away he drove toward Salem. The man asked me my name and I told him. Then a Voice said to me, *"What are you doing in this stranger's car?"* The Voice was not the man driving the car, the Voice I heard was as clear as I knew it was the Holy Spirit. I learned in reading the Bible at Church that the Holy Spirit will lead and guide us to all truth. It was then I realized I had gotten in the car with a stranger. Suddenly the fear of realizing that no one knew where I was and that this man could do anything to me - rape me, kill me, take me far away, or do anything! I immediately began to pray, *"God, please protect me, save me from any hurt, harm, or danger. Please, God, I know You can do anything."* As I opened my eyes, we were slowly entering Salem. As soon as we passed the light on York Street, I quickly told the man to let me out right at the corner. I quickly pointed my finger at the first corner after the light. I was so afraid at that point that I said it again, "Let me out right at this corner!" The man slowly pulled over and stopped the car. I jumped out of the car so fast that I almost fell.

My heart was beating fast as I quickly walked uptown to the store. The first thing I said was, *"Thank you, Lord! God, I know You are real because You spoke to me and I clearly heard You. I know You heard my prayer because, God You were right there with me to protect me, rescue me, and save me as You promised in Your Word."*

When I got home, I realized I learned a big and important lesson. I felt guilty for selfishly saving my dime and not about hopping into a car with a stranger. So I did not tell my mother or anyone because I would have gotten in trouble for my selfish and dangerous decision.

But I did learn an even bigger lesson on the ride of faith which was having a personal relationship with God is truly a blessing that will save your life. I am so glad I know Him for myself and that He is my Lord and Savior. As I walked uptown, I kept thanking God and saying, *"Lord, there is nobody like You and I will forever serve You."* My mind kept imagining what horrible things could have happened if it had not been for the Lord on my side. I could imagine how no one would ever have found me as I was a young Black girl never to have thought I was with an old White man. During those times, young girls like me would not have been a priority but God did! I am so thankful that even today our God continues to watch over me and you as He says in Word in Psalms 32:8.

Psalms 32:8 – I will instruct you and teach you the way you should go. I will counsel you with my loving eyes upon you.

FAMILY HARDSHIP –
BABY BROTHER MICHAEL

When Michael was about 3 years old, I noticed that Michael loved to climb up the long stair steps and then climb down. However, one day I watched him climb up the stair steps and once he got to the top, he would breathe so hard, like he had been running a long race. That puzzled me. Sometime after that day, Michael got sick and Mom took him to the doctor. When Mom returned from the doctor's, she announced the doctor wanted to take some tests on Michael so he would have to go into the hospital the next morning.

The next morning Michael sat quietly on the couch and I felt sad that he was going into the hospital. I stood there looking at Michael, I heard a voice in my head saying, *"Kiss him because you will never see him again."* I felt alarmed and troubled as I immediately leaned down and kissed Michael on the cheek.

Michael looked at me and smacked me on my cheek and I quickly walked out the door, feeling sorrowful that my little brother had to go to the hospital. I quickly left for school feeling very sad. I pressed to focus on school to avoid the sorrow I was feeling about my little brother being sick in the hospital.

At the supper table that night, no one talked much about Michael, but there was a quietness without words that all of us were concerned about him. A day passed by and then a second day passed by and we all sat at the supper table as usual but very little to say. Then on the 3rd day, I recalled during suppertime, the phone suddenly rang and the hospital called Dad concerning Michael. We all sat quietly at the table. After Dad hung up the phone, he quietly got up and moved his chair next to Mom. Dad had never done that before and I believe we all knew as Dad sat next to Mom that something was very wrong with Michael. Michael was throwing up and the doctor had asked permission for a procedure for Michael. We all sat silently, feeling worried and sad for our little Michael. Later Michael died of an enlarged heart and some other ailments.

When I arrived home for lunch that day, Mom met me at the door and told me Michael had died and gone to Heaven. I just stood at the door weeping and in shock and pain to know I would never see my little brother alive again in our home. I immediately remembered the last kiss I gave him, thinking I would never see him again. My Mom stood heartbroken with grief and sadness as she tried to comfort me. It took great strength for my Mom to keep going, but I know when we are weak, God is our strength.

Our house was grief-stricken but we held on to God and His Promises that absent from the body is present with the Lord. I truly believe that God is with him. My father sat in the living room grieving and brokenhearted. I looked up to view Michael's picture on the wall in the corner. I looked around and noticed Dad had removed all of Michael's pictures from the room. I imagine it was just too painful to bear for a parent in such grief. It was so hard dealing with his death but we all held on to our faith in God. We believed that God called him home and that God makes no mistakes. We loved our sweet little brother, Michael Cornell Cheak. And we were going to miss him so much that it pained our hearts that Michael was gone.

As time passed, I began to rejoice in the Lord that we had baby Michael even if just for a little while. But I know Michael is in a better place. I believe it was God's will to take Michael.

Plans were made for the funeral. During those days when someone passed, the "Viewing of the Person was in the family's home." So when family, friends, and neighbors came to our house they went into our Front Room to view Michel's body. I remembered how afraid I was to see him lying there and I just did not want to go and see Michael like that. So I began to pray and ask God to help me get through this experience. Finally, as I moved toward the casket, I looked and a feeling of relief came over me as his face did not look anything like my sweet little brother. I breathed a shy of relief as his face and complexion looked like someone else, and his hair was not done anything like the way we braided his hair so I was relieved to not recognize him at that moment. But suddenly, I looked down at his hands and sure enough they were Michael's hands. Yes, it was Michael but I believed God heard my prayer and shielded me from my fear of seeing him but confirmed that those hands were Michael's. I left the room in peace that only the Lord could give me and I was so thankful to my Lord and Savior.

After the funeral, I had a dream that I walked into our church and Michael's casket was sitting there in front of the pulpit. I quietly walked toward the casket and suddenly Michael sat up and got out of the casket. I stood in silence watching him, then he looked at me and said, "Diane, I am all right," and he turned and walked into the side room and closed the door. I suddenly woke up from the dream but with great peace and assurance that God was comforting me with a blessed assurance that Michael was with Him. Peace was with me from then on. And I thanked God for his love and comfort.

<u>SENIOR YEAR IN HIGH SCHOOL</u>

Throughout school, I got good grades and followed the rules. As graduation grew near I met with my Guidance Counselor who asked me what I wanted to do after I graduated. I smiled with confidence telling him I wanted to go to college and become a teacher. My advisor leaned back in his chair putting his hands behind his head and said, "Diane, you are not college material, you need to go to a trade school. My heart sank with disappointment as I walked out of his office. I wanted to cry.

I suddenly remembered all the things my father said and I lifted my head high and said to myself. My counselor doesn't know me and he can't tell me who I am. I believe my father when he said, "If I work hard, and live right, God can make the impossible things possible. So I held my head up and smiled because I trusted that God would make a way for me.

That day I remember sitting on the bus ride home, feeling angry at my Guidance Counsellor. Then I remembered how my Dad shared with us at the dinner table how he needed a good job so badly that he would go early in the morning and stand at the DuPont Deepwater gate hoping to be selected to get a job with benefits and steady money to provide for his family. Dad went week after week but one Sunday Morning he listened and trusted God to provide for him. Dad only had 50 cents to his name and that would probably get a week's worth of food but he took that 50 cents and put it in the offering plate. Dad said peace fell in his spirit as he trusted God to provide for him. The following Monday as he stood in line, the supervisor selected him for a job. My father worked at that DuPont job for over 30 years and retired from Dad said, "We can Trust God and I want your children to trust Him because He cannot fail." As I rode home, I knew that God would make a way for me in His own time and in His own way. God cannot fail. He is faithful and I trust the Lord.

As I listened, my faith continued to grow and I knew that things would work out for me because I had faith that I had to keep doing what was right and God wanted the best for me. I continued to think positively and kept doing my best.

FIRST PROM

My parents allowed us to go to the movies, house parties, school dances, etc. But Dad always told us to "Stay together!" One night we went to a dance at the Salem Armory across from our high school. It was jamming and students from Penns Grove, Bridgeton, and Woodstown were having a ball. On that particular night, I met a handsome guy from Penns Grove named Jimmy and he could dance so well. We had a ball dancing the crossfire and the twist. After the dance, he asked for my phone number, and of course, I was happy to give him my number.

Jimmy called me the next day and I was so happy we got to know each other. We talked a lot on the phone for hours and he told me he had broken up with his old girlfriend which made me very happy. Then one day he asked me to go to his High School prom with him. I was elated and so excited! My dad asked a lot of questions about him and found that he worked with Jimmy's father, so my dad said they were a good family and allowed me to go to the prom with him. I was so excited as I got a beautiful new gown and I wore my hair up and I looked like a princess as he picked me up for the prom. Well, at first things went well, then all of a sudden, Jimmy kept dancing and dancing and dancing with this particular girl. I asked another girl I knew about her and low and behold she said Jimmy was dancing with his old girlfriend as though he was still her boyfriend. I was so embarrassed and it looked like everyone else knew that Jimmy's old girlfriend was not going to let me take her boyfriend at her Prom and in her neighborhood. So, I knew she played me and Jimmy was falling into the trap but he did not care how I felt as he danced the night away. I was so hurt and embarrassed, but I acted like I did not see them and I could not wait until I got in the car to let him know how I felt. I mean I realized he was acting like a little boy in love and I was through with him! To make matters worse, Jim's dad heard about it and told my Dad all about how his son treated me and he apologized to my Dad for his son's behavior. And my Dad told me all about it at the supper table. But since I told my sisters what happened. I was OK as Dad spoke about it.

At that time I began to think about the kind of boyfriend I wanted in the future or even the kind of husband I would choose. I asked myself what characteristics I need to be aware of in the future. I realized I wanted a man who was honest, mature, and someone caring about my feelings. And someone like my Dad! Someone who was wise and who loved God and was thoughtful and caring and had integrity. I did not ever want to be in a situation like that again with someone so immature and oblivious to my feelings. I had to pay attention when guys talk about their past because that would tell me more about the way they deal with others. That bad situation opened my eyes and helped me to know how to pray for my future husband.

AFTER GRADUATION -
SALEM TECHNICAL INSTITUTE

After high school graduation in 1967, our parents always expected us to get a job, or go to school somewhere, so they would buy us girl's luggage and the boys a watch. Major, my oldest brother, did not graduate but left home and became a construction worker, Carl graduated and joined the Air Force and traveled the world. Naomi worked at a sewing factory and later got married, had 5 children, and became a Daycare Director. All of my older siblings were a blessing to my life and I thank God for them and although they are gone I know they knew the Lord.

Both Joann and I went to Atlantic City with our oldest brother, Major, and worked the summer after high school graduation and paid our way through a one-year course at Salem Technical Institute. Joann graduated and became an LPN nurse and I graduated as a Medical Secretary. After graduating from Salem Technical in 1968, there were no openings in the Medical field, so I was hired by Salem Technical Institute in payroll. I was still living at home in Quinton, where there was little opportunity for work, so I accepted the position in Payroll. As I learned the job, I found that I hated dealing with numbers and that kind of work.

The campus was in the country and it was so boring.

Each day I grew more and more lonely and unhappy. At times I felt I would die of loneliness. I often cried myself to sleep feeling that my life was empty. But I prayed often asking God to open a door for me to fulfill my dreams of becoming a teacher. Time dragged along but I made the best of every situation. About a year later, I still expected God would open another door for me to be a teacher like my favorite 4th-grade teacher, Ms. Zoblec, who helped me so much. She was wonderful! She made a big impact on my life and gave me self-confidence and self-worth. That's what I wanted to do for others too.

My mind recalled when I was in the 4th grade and I told my parents I wanted to go to college and be a teacher, just like Ms. Zoblec. And money was scarce at that time. As I sat on the porch I began to think about God and how I knew He could do anything! Because I knew without a shadow of a doubt that God had enough power and access, to send me to college. As I sat and closed my eyes I prayed:

Dear Lord Jesus, You are the true and living God and I thank You for all my blessings. I am asking You to send me to college to be a teacher and help children learn to have a better life. I love You Lord and thank You again for everything. Amen

PRAYER ANSWERED

I had been working at Salem Tech in payroll for about 1 year. Then it happened! My prayer was answered! I instantly knew the Lord had answered my prayer. It happened like this:

One day as I was eating lunch at a table with two co-workers, suddenly the Salem Tech Guidance Counselor approached our table with a big smile on his face asking us, "How would I like to go to college free?" I was so excited, as I knew it was my prayer being answered. I jumped at the opportunity as I asked the Counselor what I must do and where was the college. The Guidance Counselor smiled and told me it was Cumberland Community College, in Vineland, NJ, and that he would provide me with the paperwork to move forward.

I sat at lunch and could not wait to talk to the Counselor in more detail later. After work, I followed through with the paperwork and I thanked the Guidance Counselor with a smile, thinking to myself, "My high school counselor told me I was not college material." But now the Lord sent my Salem Tech counselor to offer me College and a free scholarship, just like I asked the Lord. That was straight from the Lord, I believed. I was so thankful to the Lord for his faithfulness.

My whole world changed from loneliness to happiness and excitement! I immediately knew this was the door the Lord had opened for me to go to college. I remembered my prayer asking God to provide the way for me to go to college and the access to go. He did!! I was so happy! Yet the words of my father echoed, "Never quit, always finish whatever you start." I knew if God opened the door, God would equip me to finish college. I just thanked God constantly for blessing me. The counselor gave me all the information to complete and I waited to hear the response but so far, I heard nothing from them. Meanwhile, I applied for another job at Atlantic City Hospital when my sister and I went there a little while ago. Also, I had always wanted to be an X-ray technician at Cooper Hospital as a student. So far I have not heard from any of them. I was beginning to worry as I had not heard from any of them and time was moving past.

Then one day my brother, Carl, had just called and said he was stopping over so I asked him to pick up the mail as he came by the Post Office. Carl finally got there and there in the mail were three letters. I opened the first:

1. Atlantic City Hospital offered me a position to assist the social worker at an entry-level salary.

2. Cooper Hospital accepted me as a student for X-Ray

Technician Training. They sent details of the cost of the course.

3. Cumberland Community College offered me a full scholarship.

I was overflowing with excitement but I had to consider all the options. I knew deep down in my heart, I prayed to God to allow me to go to college. But I have all three choices at one time. Just then I told my brother, Carl, and he said, "Go to college, I only wish I had that opportunity. All the other jobs and options can wait. Opportunity only knocks once! Take it, you have a chance that you may never get again! I only wish I had the opportunity to go to college, there would be no doubt what I would do! I was, happy, nervous, and excited all at the same time.

I thought of the Pros and Cons of each:

1. I considered the job in Atlantic City but I would have to rent a place and the salary was much lower than I expected.

2. Then with Cooper Hospital, I don't have enough money to pay the tuition and get a Car with Insurance to travel to and from Camden.

3. But with Cumberland College, I knew a few people who are going there I could ride with so I checked with them, and low and behold, they said they would pick me up since

they were going too!

Well, considering all of the pros and cons I decided to go Cumberland Community College, Vineland, NJ since everything fell into place from the money to the transportation to get there. Because I had no car, Kenny J. and Babes S. agreed to take me to and from school since they drove right past my house. For extra money, I worked part-time in the Administration Office.

<u>CUMBERLAND COLLEGE</u>

I even tried out for the cheerleading team and I became the first Black cheerleader at Cumberland Community College and I loved it! My whole life had turned around to Joy as the Lord blessed me.

My mind went back to my prayer to the Lord as I sat on my front porch when I was 9 years old. I looked up and I thanked God for answering my prayer to go to College free to become a teacher. My faith expanded like air in a balloon in knowing how great and real a God we serve. Psalms 84:11-12 came to mind.

The Lord God is my Sun and my Shield, the Lord God gives Grace and Glory, and No good thing will he withhold to them that walk up. Blessed is He that Trusted in the Lord.

At Cumberland Community College I met Ella, Freddie, Vickie, and a host of new friends that enriched my life. The friends I made continued to be friends even to this day. I loved college and it was one of the happiest times I ever had. My trust in God had grown as I thanked Him for answering my prayer. In my last semester, I struggled with shorthand because I had never had it before. To make matters worse, I had to pass, or I would not graduate with my class!

I was in a very hard place but I studied and prayed and trusted the Lord could help me as I reminded God how He heard my prayers as a young girl and He blessed me and I know He will equip me to achieve my goal.

I truly wanted to make my parents proud that I opened the door that they both had been denied entry into their early education. This door would open many opportunities for our family and our people. I remembered this verse that has carried me a long way. Psalms 23:11 says, "The Lord God is my sun and my shield, the Lord God gives grace and glory and no good thing will He withhold to them that walk upright. Blessed is he that Trust in the Lord."

Then, one night I prayed to the Lord to open my mind and my spiritual eyes to help me see those shorthand strokes as words just like reading a book. Glory to God, as I took the final test the next day everything came alive as I saw those shorthand strokes as words. It was amazing! I passed the test! Words cannot express how thankful I was to the Lord! God gave me such unspeakable JOY!

COLLEGE GRADUATION!

Finally, on that beautiful, hot summer day in June 1971, after two and a half years of learning, listening, practicing, absorbing, and pursuing to achieve my goal, I stood anxiously awaiting to hear my name be called to move forward to receive my College Degree. I remember smiling and holding my head high with butterflies in my stomach as my Mom, Dad, and my older sister, Naomi, watched me walk across the stage. I was so proud to have earned my associate degree from Cumberland Community College.

I felt like I walked through a door of opportunity that opened a whole new world that was now available to me and my family! I was so proud to be the first of Eugene and Ruth Cheak's family to earn a College Degree. I knew this would enrich us all. That was a day that changed all of our lives and encouraged even my friends to keep moving forward to their dreams and goals. I knew at that moment the Lord smiled on us and how so very thankful I was to Him for His Faithfulness to His Word! Little did I realize how this opened the door to future generations far beyond our immediate family. My good friend, Jane returned to get her High School Diploma and went on to get her ministerial license, both my daughters and granddaughters all have their College Degrees.

God is Awesome.

After graduation, we celebrated and rejoiced together. I thought to myself, *"Now I have finished college and the future was waiting for me."* I now had total confidence in God that my future was moving forward.

I asked God, What's the next step in this journey, God? Because I know He has a plan for me and I want Him to Lead and Guide me where He wants me to go and this scripture came to mind Jeremiah 29:11.

Jeremiah 29:11: I have a plan for you says the Lord, a plan for good and not evil, a place for a future and an expected end.

TEACHER'S JOB, NEW HOME AND
MOVING TO DELAWARE

That same year I graduated in 1971, my sister Naomi, told me there was a teaching position at her workplace. She lived and worked in Old New Castle. I was excited about applying for a Head Start position as a teacher at St. Peters School but I must admit I was nervous during the interview for the job. But low and behold I got the Job!!!! I was so excited and happy. I could hardly believe how everything was falling into place so perfectly. God Blessed me to become a TEACHER! Halleluiah!

Now that I had a job, I needed a place to live and Old New Castle was a nice quaint little town. My sister and I drove around and we happened to see her old realtor as we were looking at the neighborhood. Surprisingly, he said he had row houses he was going to rent and that he would show them to us. When he took us to the house it was located at 67 W. Fourth Street, in Old New Castle, right around the corner to the school. This could not have been a more perfect location to live. When he showed me the house with a small living room, two upstairs bedrooms, and a large room right off from the kitchen, and when he said the rent was only $80 per month, I almost fainted with joy as it was perfect!! To make it even more wonderful, my house was right next to Battery Park and the Tennis Court. The church was a block away for me to walk to on Sundays. No one but God could have laid things out so perfectly and I was so thankful to Him.

Well, I not only got the house, but my dad took me to buy furniture for my first house. Since he knew the furniture managers, we got a great deal on a living room set and a bedroom set for my room. They made payment arrangements and it all worked out great. Not to mention my paycheck was more than enough to pay all my bills and have savings as well. Words of thank you could not be enough to the Lord for it all.

First of all, the school was two blocks from my house and I had many good experiences teaching preschool children at Head Start. The children were very precious, honest, talkative, and extremely active. The more I worked with them the more I learned about the different little personalities and the many ways to help children learn and enjoy learning. I always observed and wondered about people and the "Why" they were this way or that way. I found it helped me to see and understand more specific ways to help children. I knew that every experience impacts children's lives and affects their personality and self-esteem in their early years. I continuously prayed that they would be blessed to be a blessing to others.

When I told my sister-in-law, Jill, about my moving to Delaware she got excited. She married my brother Carl and had a son they named Joseph Carl Cheak, Jr. but we called him "Bubbles." When Bubbles was about three years old, my brother and Bubbles were in a serious car accident and my brother Carl died but Bubbles survived. After the accident, his wife, Jill, and her son needed a change after the loss. Since we were very good friends and I told her about the house I found, she wanted to come and join me. So Jill and Bubbles moved in with me. That worked out well as Jill met our neighbor Ms. Roberts and they became good friends.

Soon I met a friend across the street who also taught in another preschool teacher named, Charlotte. She became one of my best friends. While attending that church a block away from my house, I met Evelyn Chandler who also became one of my best friends. Evelyn lived down the Street and she and I often visited her as we sat on her porch for hours laughing and sharing the many ways God had blessed us.

I often went to Battery Park which was right across the street where large ships and Speed Boat would sail down the Delaware River. Often we watched beautiful swarms of ducks swimming along the shore. I also found the people on 4th street were very nice and friendly too. Old New Castle was exactly the perfect place for me to live. It had a quaint and country atmosphere that was very inviting.

On Sundays, I went to church around the corner and the people were friendly and the pastor and his wife welcomed me. And with it all, I knew God answered my prayer with this teaching position and that is why everything fell into place. I sat in amazement as God opened doors of opportunity to me one after one. I was so very thankful and there was such a peace in my home that words could not have.

<u>MEETING MY HUSBAND</u>

To explain how grateful I was I got on my knees and prayed to God that I would fulfill the purpose He had for me in this beautiful world He made. And just as I had asked God, "What was the next chapter in my life, little did I know how life-changing the following year would be for me. 1972 Here I Come!

It was a bright sunny day in October of 1971 when I was visiting my best friend Ella while stopping to see her sister, Freddie, and her husband Stanley. I was introduced to Sumblar Carroll, but he said most people called him Skip. Ella leaned over in the car to whisper she had recently met Skip as he walked our way. I noticed how he smiled as he approached Ella and me while sitting in Ella's car. I liked his smile and his caring voice as he kindly spoke to us. He was very appealing to me. When he turned to walk away, I watched him walk with a sense of pride and purpose. There was something different about him that I found very attractive. At that moment, he turned and looked back at me with a smile on his face as though he knew I was watching him. His warm glance made me feel special. I found him interesting and very appealing.

When Ella and I returned to her house, Skip had wasted no

time in calling my friend Ella asking to speak with me. I was elated as he showed interest in me. Skip asked if Ella and I would like to come over later that evening to socialize with Freddie and Stanley's brothers. Both Ella and I agreed since we had no plans for the evening. When we arrived, we heard the latest sound of "Isaac Hayes and Hot Butter and Soul" album as we entered the house. We all greeted each other and sat and talked, danced, and sipped our mixed drinks to the mellow sounds of Aretha Franklin, Marvin Gaye, and other popular tunes. Ms. Tibbs was there frying delicious chicken and we all enjoyed eating and socializing in such a relaxing atmosphere. We left feeling very good about our evening.

Surprisingly, when we arrived home Skip asked me if he could take me to church the next day, to which I happily agreed, and with a smile, I was impressed with his interest in me. When he picked me up for church the next day, he was so well dressed in a brown suit, white shirt, and a black tie and he was such a gentleman as he opened the car door for me and treated me like a queen. This guy was very different from anyone I met. Yes, I thought to myself, *"This guy has great potential and initiative,"* and I was very, very impressed.

After church, I told him I was going to call my Dad to take

me back to New Castle, Delaware. Skip said, "I'll take you to Delaware!" with a big smile on his face. I was surprised and reluctant for him to take me all the way home and I had not known him very long. So I asked my friend Ella and she said, He's really a nice guy you can trust him. I thought about it and felt he was a gentleman and I let Skip drive me back home to Delaware. I felt so comfortable as we rode.

Skip called me the following day and asked me what I was doing the following week, I told him I was taking the bus to Atlantic City. He immediately said to me, "I'll take you to Atlantic City!" I was shocked that he was so nice to me! This guy was getting all kinds of points for making me feel like a "Queen" and I loved it! And he was making me so happy. He was a perfect gentleman and very honest and kind and that went a long way for me.

The next day he called me and we talked for hours on the phone. I discovered that Skip lived and worked with Bobby, Billy, and Stanley Tibbs painting houses. Skip's family were very creative and ambitious and lived in Bridgeton. There was always something to talk about and Skip and I would often go to Duncan Donuts and sit for hours laughing and talking about any and everything.

As our friendship grew Skip moved from New Jersey to Delaware. He rented a room at the YMCA and shortly after arriving, he found a job. Then he could come over to my house and he cooked us a pork chops dinner. He was a good cook but two people cannot eat 21 pork chops in one meal. But we laughed and joked about it. Skip was often very creative in making something old and ugly to look new and beautiful. He always made dull times, fun times that's why I loved being with him. Skip was very ambitious and he started going to OIC to learn a new trade, and I ended up going with him to OIC and they helped both of us land a good job. It was then I found in Delaware it's all about who you know, not what you know.

ENGAGED

One cold winter day Skip worked at a job and he gave me all the money he made and then bought me a pair of beautiful gloves to keep my hands warm. Well now that loving act of kindness stole my heart and I fell in love with Skip. Our relationship moved quickly and in 6 months from the time I met Skip, he asked me to marry him! I was happy and shocked and little did I know, Skip had gone to my Father and asked permission to marry me! I was so happy and I was so thankful he did. I always felt that was the right and respectable thing to do.

I immediately began planning the wedding and three months later we were all set to be man and wife on June 17, 1972. The wedding was just 9 months after we met and along with our family and friends, everything moved forward very nicely.

I told my mother and father and they jumped in to help. My Dad brought Ms. Tunis the organist at our home church over from New Jersey to Delaware to practice for the wedding. Dad and Mom gave me money for the food. Ms. Tibbs, Bobby, Billy, and Stanley's Mom made the table centerpieces for the tables at the church basement where our first reception would be. Then Sandy and Jessie gave us another reception at their home with

Jessie's father and his wife to share in our celebration. Maud did my hair free and beautiful. Naomi made my veil, gave me a Bridal Shower at her house, and helped me decorate the church. Pauline picked Roses from her garden and placed them in the Church windows, they were beautiful. Sandy lent me her Beautiful Wedding Gown, size 7, and fits me perfectly.

My young nephew, Lemont, was my ring bearer. Bobby, Billy, and Jessie were the Best Men, and Joann was my Maid of Honor, with Sandy and Pauline. It was a beautiful coming together as family and friends. I was so happy.

I never could have imagined that my life would change so rapidly but it did. I prayed much and was very thankful to the Lord that he had blessed me with a job I have always wanted, a house that I could afford, a nice country-friendly neighborhood with a church, the park, the library, and nice country folks that made me feel safe and at home. I truly thanked God for answering my prayers.

THE WEDDING DAY

When I awoke on my wedding day, June 17th, it rained like cats and dogs! I could not believe it! But, Glory to God by noon the sun was shining, all the rain had dried up and it was a beautiful day. I was excited as I put on my beautiful gown and everyone was at the church. However, no one thought to have a car pick me up since the church was a block away. So as I stepped out of the door, I felt like Cinderella as the entire neighborhood stood watching me walk to the church as the bride-to-be. I felt like I was in a dream as everyone cheered me on.

When I arrived at the church, my Father was standing there waiting to give me away. I remember thinking to myself, "Self, how do you feel?" A Peace fell over me and I knew this commitment was forever. The church door opened and my father walked me down the aisle. I saw my family and friends welcoming me with smiling faces. Beautiful flowers were placed in the windows of the church and was decorated beautifully. And there stood Sumblar in his white suit standing like a soldier, looking at me as Jessie and Bobby and the others stood next to him.

As the Preacher proceeded with the ceremony, asking

Sumblar if he would take me as his wife, he stood frozen in silence so long that I nudged him to respond and he said, "I DO!" Everybody laughed and so did I as we proceeded with our vows. Finally, we were pronounced, Husband and Wife as we turned to walk from the church. I was stepping into a new life journey as Mrs. Sumblar Carroll.

We were married on a Saturday, June 17, 1972, and our good friends, Sandy, and Jessie, had a party at their house along with the other four couples we hung around with and enjoyed. It was a day to remember and I could not have had a more beautiful wedding day. Later that night we had three carloads of friends that drove to Atlantic City and went to the "Reggie Edgehill's Persian Room" and danced the night away. We stayed overnight, my sister Joann treated us to breakfast and then we drove home. That was the honeymoon. And I was so satisfied and happy!!!

My wedding day was more than I ever dreamed it would be and I am so thankful that these memories will live on as I share these stories with my family and friends.

BACK TO WORK

Since I had only been on my job at Hercules Inc. for two weeks, they only gave me a day off for my wedding so on Monday morning, I went back to work in the Purchasing Department. However, Skip had just got laid off his job the day before our wedding and I said to him, "I am not going to let anything rain on my Wedding Day! So I told him to put it out of your mind and let's have the best weekend ever! We had the best Wedding and the wedding reception was also wonderful. A few weeks later, Skip got a job at the Bank of Delaware as a proof operator and things went well. He worked there for many years until he moved up to become a Bank Teller.

Married life began with ups and downs, but I relied on my faith in God that He would fix it and I knew He would work things out and he did. Skip got a puppy a few months before we were married and he named him Chadow. Skip spent a lot of time with Chadow along with him teething and Skip was still training him. Chadow even chewed the legs off my recorder stand and messed all over the house. I was so upset! But I found these were only minor ups and downs of marriage. Thank God Chadow began to grow on me and he was a beautiful dog.

I realized when I was a teacher it's best to start with marriage by just enjoying and learning each other's ways before having a family. We decided to hold off from a family and just learn and enjoy each other. We enjoyed each other and had so many wonderful times having parties in our Black Room at 67 W. 4th Street. Later Skip became a Disc Jockey, known as Super Jock Sherlock. He played all over Delaware and New Jersey. We had shows with guests like Jerry Wells from WDAS, a popular radio station in Philadelphia. He also modeled with Melba's Models from Philly and we had fashion shows with the latest outfits!

For three years we had no children and we went everywhere with a nickel in our pockets. Because we never had much money we were determined to make the best of any situation. We would go to Atlantic City with a full tank of gas with only $5.00 in our pockets as we visited my sister, Joann.

Our friends, Jessie & Sandy, Lucille & Darnell, Country & Maud, and a few other couples would take turns having a party at each other's house. Sumblar also painted a Black Room in our house to party and entertain with friends. My husband always had a creative idea to do something to improve our home. We had good times and I thanked God for the wonderful times we had in those early years of marriage. Life was good!

During those first three years, I noticed how ambitious and

creative Sumblar was in whatever he had a mind to do. Sumblar always strived to be the best of whatever she did. So one day, he and I were sitting at our favorite spot at Duncan Donuts and I said to him, Remember when I first met you and I looked at you and smiled. He smiled back and said he remembered that day. I told him I always liked the way he walked and I immediately felt he had "Great Potential" in whatever work he pursued because he always took pride in whatever he did and he wanted to be the best. That's why I was not surprised when he worked at the Bank of Delaware as a proof operator, later he said he wanted to advance to a bank teller. He did well as a teller, then he became such a popular DJ that he worked the next 7 years as a full-time DJ, Super Jock Sherlock. Yes, life was full of plenty of things to do and places to go. Life was good!

WHAT? MOVING TO OUR APARTMENT

Just four months after we were married Sumblar came home and stated we were going to move to Haverford Place Apartments on Limestone Road. I was surprised he found a place but when he told me how much the rent was I was shocked because it was so much higher than what we were paying for the house on 67 West 4th Street where we were paying $80 per month for a whole house and now Sumblar was telling me our rent would be $149 per month. I went to the roof! That was $69 more a month more than what we were paying. Our money was scarce and with a rent increase was over my head. But Skip was very excited about the apartment so he took me to look at it. Yes, it was nice and I must admit I loved it! But when Skip stated that now we can have a place that is "Both ours not just yours." Well, all along Skip said it did not matter that we lived in the house that "I had" before we were married, but he revealed it did matter! Because of his feelings, I agreed to move to Haverford Place Apartments. I must admit, I loved the place, the people, the location, and everything.

During the many years we lived there I had all kinds of friends like Penny, Barbara, Angie, Mildred, Angel, Melva and so many other nice people. It was just like a family at Haverford Place.

We women would get together often as we all were struggling financially yet finding ways to enjoy both ourselves and our children's lives. Yes, we had such wonderful memories at Haverford Place.

Three years later, we had our first child, Seliques Diane Carroll. She was beautiful, smart, and creative like her father. Then 7 years later April, she was beautiful, loving, and creative. Things went pretty well as we had birthday parties and all the friend and their kids came over for ice cream and cake along with talking and just having a good time. Kids were sleeping over at each other's apartment and things were good living at Haverford Place for the last 13 years.

Then around 1984 new neighbors moved in with dogs, cats, and all kinds of loud music. But now the rent was $750 per month and I could not find peace in my own house. I was fed up with complaining and I planned to move so I got a large cardboard box and placed it in the walk-in closet as my hope chest. So that anything I found for my new house I would buy and place in my hope chest.

SEARCHING TO BUY A NEW HOME

From this time I drove around the neighborhood searching for the right house for us and slowly planning to move somewhere we could enjoy and call our own home. Surprisingly, I met a new friend at church who was looking for a new home too. She told me she had a great realtor and gave me his name and I contacted him. However, my girls and I continued searching neighborhoods for our dream house and suddenly we found the exact house we wanted in Overview Gardens. My daughter Seliques and I were so excited we jumped out of the car and left April who was three years old in the car crying as we stood marveling at the perfect house for our family. I had made up my mind I would pray and ask God to give us that house and I did, believing that would make a way for us. Later I found out I could not afford the house and soon after I drove passed the house and there was a SOLD sign on it. I was so very disappointed but I knew I could not afford it.

I continued to look at another house which was Choice #2 and I shared this with my friend at Church. She suggested that I "Fast and Pray" and allow God to give me the right house. So I did and I trusted God to give me what was best for me. I also took my husband to see the house and he was not excited at all about it but agreed to be supportive. Well, I prayed and fasted for three days and I drove by the house each day. On the third day, I went by the house and a big "SOLD" sign was on it! I was shocked and upset and I immediately realized God said "No" so I accepted what his answer was for me.

Immediately, I called my Realtor Rocky, and told him that I saw the sign on the house he showed us. Rocky confirmed it was "SOLD" free and clear. Then Rocky said, "Ms. Carroll, don't you worry, I have 5 houses to show you on Saturday, will you be free to look at them? I said, Yes and agreed to meet at 10 am to look at other homes. I was rather disappointed at this time but I decided to keep going,

On Saturday morning, Rocky took me to the various homes but it was either the right house but, the wrong neighborhood or the house was too small or not my style of home. I was beginning to get frustrated and discouraged as we had already looked at 4 houses in different neighborhoods. My hope of finding the right house was fading by now. So I silently waited to arrive at the last house on our list.

OUR DREAM HOME

Finally, we were down to the 5th and last house to see. and when we drove up to the house it was my First Choice, The Dream House. I was shocked as I sat in the car! I knew I could not afford it, so I said to Rocky, "Why would you bring me to this house because I know I cannot afford it! Rocky, "Do you know that this is the "Dream House" I wanted but I cannot afford it and it was also "SOLD" and I was annoyed and disappointed as I sat there refusing to move.

Then Rocky looked at me with a smile and said, "I am not showing you any house you cannot afford, because you are qualified for the First Time Homeowner Bond money. I paused and said, "What is BOND MONEY?" He said it's a program you qualify for as a First Time Homeowner, so let's go in!

Once inside, 59 Briarcliff Drive, I fell in love with the house. The Lady who owned the house told me she loved the house, but her new husband bought her a new home. I also asked her, "Didn't someone buy this house when you had the house up for Sale a short while ago?" She said, "Yes, but things did not work out." I was so pleased with the house I could not wait to show my husband the place.

Once I showed the house to my husband, he loved it and was

sold on getting it. Then after sharing my good news with another co-worker, she said, "You know you qualify for the First Time Home Buyer Program as an employee." I said, "What are you talking about?" She said, "Call Human Resources and ask them about the program." I did just that and I received another $5000 toward buying our Dream Home. I was so thankful to the Lord, words could not express my joy and appreciation.

But out of nowhere, there was one last glitch in my joy that I never thought about. I had taken out $1100 from my savings to pay off my car to decrease any upcoming bills. Suddenly, Rocky called me and said they saw that $1100 was missing from our savings. I explained I paid off the car. Rocky said, "Diane you must have that $1100 back in your account according to all your paperwork today or we cannot go to settlement and now you need a gift letter to show it was not a loan." I was shocked with fear of not getting my dream house. Then I thought to myself, *"My Dad is the only one that I can ask for the money but he lives in New Jersey."* I called him right away, and he quickly said, "Yes, I can do that for you."

So, I told my supervisor I had an emergency and left work quickly heading to New Jersey. When I arrived at my Dad's house, Dad handed me 11 one-hundred-dollar bills and signed the gift letter. I said Dad how did you get to the bank so quickly? He said he had it just sitting in his desk since he did not want to send his car payment all at one time. I smiled and hugged him and Mom as I left to deposit the $1100 in my savings account at the Credit Union. Then I hurried back to the Credit Union Supervisor who told me she would open the door and make the deposit in my savings, so I could take the receipt to Rocky to confirm the settlement was still set as planned. After all this was done, all I could say was, "I love you Lord Jesus, and I thank you for being so good to me! I praised and gave all glory to my Lord and Savior as I rejoiced to praise our Great Lord and Savior for all He has done for me. I share that testimony at every opportunity.

MOVING IN OUR DREAM HOME

We moved into our Dream House at 59 Briarcliff Drive on February 28, 1985, and I felt like I had always lived there. Just the atmosphere of the house was so inviting as though we were finally in the home that God chose for us to live. Truly He orchestrated all of this and He answered my first prayer as only He can do. Sumblar and the kids loved the house and all our friends and family came to celebrate with us.

Once we moved in Sumblar and one of his friends painted the entire house. He then put new wall-to-wall rugs in the larger rooms. Now there was a huge pine tree in our front yard that was crooked and it stood tall and leaning in the air. My father noticed the pine tree right away and he stood and looked at it and said to Skip, cut it down, it's an eye sore and you don't want it falling on your home. Skip stood looking at the tree also commenting. Then Skip started digging up the landscape and he planted beautiful plants and flowers to enhance the yard. Sometime later, I came home and Skip had cut the top off the tree, trimmed the leaves, and cut the bottom branches off, then painted the trunk of the tree white and that tree was the most beautiful tree you want to have standing on our front yard. I was amazed at how beautiful it looked and Skip said, "I remember The Karate Kid Movie where the trees were shaped like that and I made one for us." What a gift Skip had for making something plain, old, or ugly into something beautiful.

BACK TO COLLEGE

Several years later, I decided to go back to school to get my bachelor's degree at Wilmington College. Hercules paid for the course if I passed with a "C" or above. My advisor instructed me to first take the accounting class. I had never had accounting and the class was overcrowded it was the first time in 20 years I was back in college. Well, I worked hard and got the basic idea but little did I know that half the class had failed the course and was taking it over. Then as I was on break one day, I overheard the teacher talking as he stated "In my class, you either get an A or an F, there is no in-between. Well, I thought I was doing well in the first half of the semester as the class continued to decrease in size. I thought I had passed, but when I called to find out my final grade I was told that I "Failed" the class. I was devastated! I had never failed a class in my life. My self-esteem was injured and I was shocked as I sat alone and felt great shame as I cried. I asked myself, *"Who can I tell?"* The only person I could think of who would still love me was Sumblar. I called him and told him as I cried that I did not pass the class. I could not even say the word "failed." Sumblar said, "Diane you are a winner and don't you dare let anyone tell you any difference. I thanked him and hung up the phone as I sat at my desk, still weeping, and hurt. A short while later, Sumblar came to my desk carrying a beautiful bouquet of flowers, and with such a loving smile, he kissed me and said, "You are a winner, and don't let anyone ever tell you anything else. He then sat on my lap, hugged me, told me to dry my eyes and said, "You are a Winner," as he left to return to work. He was such a comfort to me in my bruised self-esteem.

Little did Sumblar know, how deeply hurt I was but God knew. After my pity party, I prayed and began to realize it was God who got my attention for a reason. He knew I was beginning to think I was self-sufficient. Like I could do anything and God knocked me down because He knew I needed to meet some people who could put me on the path He had for me. But first and foremost, I needed to depend on Him for everything. God knew I thought that a bachelor's degree was not going to lead me to the plan and path He had for me. So, God put a "Holt" on it all.

Sometime later in building my self-esteem and speaking skills, I attended a Toastmaster's Meeting. Just as I entered the meeting, Evelyn Tyson stood up at the Lectern as she delivered a presentation entitled, Let Your Life Count." The words, the message, and the presentation actually ministered to me and I felt so uplifted and rejuvenated in her speech. It touched me to think about what life was all about. I felt I was back on track and as Evelyn finished her presentation, I met her and shortly afterward we became very close friends I called her my Spiritual Mother as she was so wise in the Lord. Evelyn was legally blind, she worked and God gifted her with a beautiful voice that she used to minister to others. God also passed a gift to her daughter, Beverly, who also sang songs of praise. I think either Evelyn or Beverly sang at Carnegie Hall in New York. But they loved and served the Lord in spreading the Good News of Jesus Christ.

JOBLESS BUT NOT HOPELESS

After working Hercules for 17 years there was a job downsizing. They gave me a choice of going with a Subsidiary Company of Hercules and losing all my 17 years to start at the bottom or take a severance package and move on to another job. I prayed about it and I decided I was not going to panic and make a decision in fear but I was going to pray and trust God. After much prayer, I elected to move on and trust God. Once I told my supervisor my decision, a great peace filled my heart, it was confirmation to me that I had made the right choice. I then went directly to my husband at his beauty salon and told him. He was surprised but knew as long as I was alright, he was too. He said, "I'm good 'cause I'm with you." With my severance pay, I had time to search for a job but I also had time to pray and get things in order. I applied at St. Francis Hospital, FMC, and various other businesses. I was very specific in praying for a job because I learned to be specific with Him. FMC was my first choice and it had everything I wanted. They called me for a second interview and I just knew I had the job. But I did not get it. I was disappointed and I complained to God. Well, I must have been out of my head, because, God always knows what's best so I truly repented for my complaining. I called about a follow-up at St. Francis Hospital, and they said they were interviewing right at the time I called but said they never got my application. Well, I told them I submitted my application three times and I aggressively asked if I could be included in the interview. They replied yes but I had to be there by 1:00 p.m. and I did.

ST. FRANCES HOSPITAL

Interviewed for a Healthcare Delaware Rep. for the insurance program they had. The interview went well but when they told me the starting rate, I had the nerve to ask if they could increase it as I had a lot of experience and I knew I would do a good job. The interviewer looked at me like I was crazy and said the salary was probably locked in. Well, I was called back for a second interview and the Supervisor was someone I knew from Hercules Inc. She was happy to see me and the first thing she said was, "Of course you know I am giving you the increase you requested. I was so happy and we just chatted. I realized that as the Bible says, A good reputation is worth more than silver and gold. The supervisor gave me the job as a Healthcare Rep. The group was nice to work with and all my requests the Lord provided.

During that time there was much change in businesses, the economy, and inflation. Well, I was requested to inform FMC employees who were being laid off of their healthcare benefits. I was shocked that there was a big layoff because that was the company I interviewed twice for and I really wanted the job. But now they were laying off people and I thanked God He did not give me that job because I would have been job searching again,

BUT God knew all about it! I serviced the FMC Employees with compassion and kept thinking about how it could have been me.

About 8 months later Heath Care, DE was folding up too due to inflation, but we were given opportunities to work in other parts of St. Frances Hospital. I went on an interview in Human Resources, but I was told they were only giving me a courtesy interview because they had already made their choice. I went to the interview and it went so well that the Supervisor said she was changing her mind and wanted me for the position of Personnel Development assistant.

<u>EARNING MY BACHELOR'S AND</u>
<u>MASTER'S DEGREES</u>

I got the position and I thanked God because it was one of the best jobs I had in helping the entire hospital with training rooms, badges, and tuition reimbursement. And I had the best supervisor ever, Lynda Turner. When Lynda asked what my future goals were, I told her I wanted to go back to Wilmington College and get my bachelor's degree. She said that was a great idea and reminded me that St. Francis Hospital benefits would pay for my tuition and I needed to provide for the books.

So, I enrolled after a 6-year break from my last failing course I began Wilmington College. Lynda was supportive of me using our computer for term papers and coming in after work to complete them. After work I caught the bus to Wilmington College for 2 ½ years, working a full-time job, raising our children and I earned my bachelor's degree in Human Resource Management. Graduation was wonderful and Lynda came to celebrate with me and my family. I was the first family member to get my bachelor's degree and we all celebrated.

Then I saw Lynda had laid a magazine on my desk with an article circled for me to read. When I read it, I asked Lynda why she gave me the article. Lynda said, "Diane, I have watched you work hard and earn your bachelor's, and you have inspired me to go and get my master's degree and I want you to go with me too." The article proves and shows the benefits of earning our master's degree at Wilmington College together. I said I am tired of going to school. I need a break. Lynda said think about it, you are so close and you are familiar with how you manage to get things done. So I thought about it and both Lynda and I went back to Wilmington College and I earned my master's degree in Human Resource Management.

Two months after I earned my degree, St. Frances Hospital had a huge layoff. George the Director came and sat at my desk and explained my severance package in such a caring way. I kindly thanked him and went to the movie to see, "Sabrina."

I had worked there for 7 years and I was blessed that St. Frances paid for both my bachelor's and master's degrees. I was thankful for the training and the opportunity to work with so many wonderful people.

I praised God for all He provided and I looked back at my journey knowing He had ordered my steps all the way.

NEIGHBORHOOD HOUSE

Fortunately, I was hired at Neighborhood House where I was the Family Specialist who assisted mostly women and children with electric assistance, food, and clothes and as many referrals to contact other agencies to help their needs. I also worked with the city and the various programs, funds, and various agencies.

I learned and met many people and agencies that I was not aware of to help those in need. I had about 30 case clients. It was the kind of job I liked and seeing people advance and move forward in life.

I also went to the Women's prison to facilitate the Inside Out Program. When getting my master's degree I wrote a program for women incarcerated and I asked the Executive Director to read it before I submitted it. She did and she loved it and wanted to go to the Women's Prison and help the women. Because I was a Board Member of Delaware Associate for Children of Alcoholics. We went and discussed the program with the Warden and he approved it.

I ran that program for over 9 years going in 2 months in the spring and 2 months in the fall. The program truly made a difference and we even had graduation in which I asked my

Sister Naomi to come and sing at the program. Percilla, Jane, Mary, and other friends came in to be the keynote speaker. We took Polaroid pictures and had refreshments.

Some of the women came and got assistance at the location where I was working after they were released. The Program was a success.

Later I was awarded the Bank of Delaware Neighborhood Award for DaCoa for serving the women inmates to move forward in their lives.

I worked at Neighborhood House for 2 years. Then one day I received a large brown envelope with a state application in it. I applied for the Administrative Job but I had no idea who sent the application to me. However, one day Mr. Rollins called me from the hospital asking me to run the food meeting for him. I agreed then he asked if I applied for the job. I said, "Was that you who sent me that application?" "Yes," he replied, "did you hear what your score was?" "What score?" I asked. He said, "Call the state office and ask if you qualified." I did and they informed me they would be interviewing in a week or so. I prayed and asked God to show me the way and to increase my territory to help others in need.

PORTER STATE SERVICE CENTER

I was surprised, that State Service Center said they would be calling me for an interview. But they called the next week and wanted me to interview for the Administrator position. I was shocked to see five people at the long table asking me question after question. My head was spinning when I left. A day later they requested a second interview. I went and it was more difficult than the first. When I walked out of the interview, I said, *"God, it's up to you and I don't care if I get the job or not, all I know is that the interview was too much and my head is spinning. God, it's Your way, not mine."* And I did not think about it either way.

About two days later, I received a call from the State Service Center offering me the position. I immediately said, "Yes" but I had no idea what the responsibilities and challenges were for the job.

Well, I was in for a shock because Porter SSC sat right in the midst of the neighborhood and was one of the busiest and hardest of all 15 State Service Centers. I would be responsible for the safety of the Public Health and Social Services and transporting the children from school to our State Dental office. That is a lot to be in charge of I thought but I'll have to do my homework on how to manage things.

On June 1, 2000, I started the job by being trained in the Charles Debman building by our Regional Manager. She would instruct me on inputting time, submitting monthly reports, and learning to purchase staff supplies that had to be ordered and other information that Upper Management needed to be provided in a timely manner. Surely, it was a very large responsibility. But I asked God to direct me.

After a month I was sent to Porter State Service Center to get my office in order. I found the desk drawers were falling apart and the facility needed a huge upgrade. I had 10 people to supervise and one lead Worker, Tiffany, who knew her job very well. Surprisingly, there were always from 15 to 20 people standing outside in line to be serviced even before the doors opened at 8:00 a.m. I was shocked that this many people would come and stand in line, some arguing and others cussing at each other waiting for one of the three agencies at Porter State Service Center which included: Social Services, 3rd floor, Public Health-2nd floor, State Services, my floor with 8 staff members for rent assistance, food, homelessness, etc. and the basements for Dental Services for school children I was responsible for all of this along with the fire drills, client issues and staff supervision, monthly reports and staff time and evaluations. Truly, I need God!

I found this was the most challenging job I had ever had or imagined. I sat at my desk and realized only God was able to carry me through this tremendous challenge. I knew I could trust Him to lead and guide me in achieving my goals.

REMEMBERING THE BLESSINGS FROM GOD

I began remembering as I sat at my desk, how God had continually been with me and answered my prayers way back when I was a young child who would sit in church listening and learning all about God and how He made the world. Everything I learned caused me to believe that He knew everything about everybody and had all the power to do anything He chose to do. God wanted the best for us all but we have a choice in doing or not doing the right thing.

Many things in my life happened to assure me that God is real and will always be there no matter where I go and He would help me no matter how hard or difficult life issues happened in my life.

So now with this difficult job, I remembered the scripture in Philippians 4:13: "I can do all things through Christ who strengthens me."

I realize that this verse says it is Christ who has all power and I will trust and follow Him in achieving whatever goal He set before me. I knew it was God who opened the door for me to get this Administrator's position for the State of Delaware and I trusted Him to lead and guide me. Therefore, I knew I had to get on my knees every day and seek His face. So each morning I came in, closed my office door, got on my knees, prayed and I had to line up with God in whatever He wanted me to do. My faith was being strengthened and tested as I dealt with various issues with staff, other divisions in the building, and difficult clientele.

But through it all, I saw God and little did I know I would be at that job longer than any of the previous Administrators had stayed because I was told it was known to be the hardest and busiest State Service Center than most of the 15 centers.

The interesting thing is years ago I prayed to God to increase my territory to be able to help more people in more ways. God never forgot and I never expected to be at the job to help so many people and so many different ways but He never forgot! I realized it was all about God giving me wisdom, courage, and endurance to help clients who were in need.

I watched God in His perfect timing having funds to help those who had to raise grandchildren while their children were incarcerated along with those who just needed a boost to help them along. We even had a food closet downstairs for anyone in immediate need of food. Some people needed employment and I was able to hire staff and help students learn business by working a few hours to understand the real activities in business. Yes, many people have been blessed as I worked at Porter SSC.

Surprisingly, I remained at the job for 16 years and was able to retire in 2016. All I can say is Praise God for all He has done throughout my life and I am so thankful to be able to share some of my journey with you.

I pray that you are encouraged to trust and obey Him and serve the King of Kings and Lord of Lords.

THE CHEAK FAMILY TREE

My Father

Eugene Henry Cheak

Ruth Brown Cheak

Grandfather	**Grandmother**
Eugene Henry Cheak	Grace Wilson Cheak
John Brown	Ruth Brown

Eugene & Ruth Cheak hand 7 Children:

Eugene Major Cheak

Joseph Carl Cheak

Ruth Naomi Cheak

Diane Barbara Cheak

Joann Stella Cheak

Rose Marie Cheak

Michael Cornell Cheak

Children and their Grandchildren:

Eugene – Tony, Valery, Rita, Eugene, Sharon, Inkey

Carl – Joseph Carl Cheak (Bubbles)

Ruth- Michael & Michelle (Twins) Renay, Anita, and Lamont

Diane – SeLiques and April

Joann – Crystal

Rose – No children

Michael – No children

ABOUT THE AUTHOR

Evangelist Diane Cheak Carroll is the daughter of the late Reverend Eugene Henry Cheak and Ruth Brown Cheak of Haven United Methodist Church, Quinton, NJ. She has been married for 52 years to Sumblar B. Carroll, they have two beautiful daughters and five grandchildren. While raising her family, Evangelist Carroll returned to college and earned both her bachelor's and master's degrees in Human Resources Management from Wilmington University. Following receiving her master's degree. She taught Business Ethics at Wilmington University. Evangelist Carroll was also an Administrator at Porter State Service Center for 16 years and retired from the State of Delaware in 2016.

Evangelist Carroll was ordained in September 2007 but the Lord called her long before that day especially ministering to women. She and her sister, Joann, were founders of Walking in Christ Ministry for over 20 years. The mission focused on enlightening, encouraging, and empowering women in their spiritual journey. Evangelist Carroll also created the Inside/Out

Program for incarcerated women. She facilitated this program for over 12 years at Delores Baylor's Women's Correctional Institution under the sponsorship of the Delaware Association for Children of Alcoholics. She was a board member and facilitator for over 17 years. Evangelist Carroll received a "Local Hero's" award from Bank of America for sponsoring over 200 women in transitioning their lives.

Other organizations Evangelist Carroll has been a member of the Delaware Coalition Against Domestic Violence (DCADV), where she was a chairperson of the Women of Color Task Force (WOCTF), which targets faith-based organizations. WOCTF presents seminars and provides resources for preventing domestic violence. Evangelist Carroll also helped facilitate the Sunday Breakfast Mission's Women's Bible Study where lives have been changed through teaching the Good News of Jesus Christ, our Lord and Savior.

Evangelist Carroll has a calling to proclaim the Word of God, especially to women. She is a wife, sister, aunt, coworker, and friend, but most of all she is a Woman of God called to be a vessel of honor in serving the Lord. A favorite scripture she lives by is Proverbs 3:3-6.

Proverbs 3:3-6 - NIV

3 Let love and faithfulness never leave you;

bind them around your neck,

write them on the tablet of your heart.

4 Then you will win favor and a good name

in the sight of God and man.

5 Trust in the LORD with all your heart

and lean not on your own understanding;

6 in all your ways submit to him,

and he will make your paths straight.[a]